Derek
Happy christmas
Brian + Jo.

# BRISTOL'S HISTORY

## VOLUME TWO

### by

## Charles Wells

0 900814 47 0

> If I were a man of leisure, I might be tempted to write another Bristol book. It would be on the street lore of the city, tracing the history of some of the oldest streets, stating what notable man or woman lived in this or that house. Alas! that it must ever be one of the many things that I shall never be able to do. I make a present of the idea to any man who can do it, and can afford to ignore financial considerations, for such a work could not possibly be a commercial success.
>
> Charles Wells, 1921.

*The photographs taken, or collected by, and the book designed, and published by*

## REECE WINSTONE

at 23 Hyland Grove, Bristol 9

———

1975

Printed by R. J. Acford Ltd., Chichester, Sussex

# Chapters


|  |  | page |  |  | page |
|---|---|---|---|---|---|
| 11. | College Green ... ... | 102 | 14. | King Street and Prince Street | 147 |
| 12. | Park Street and Queen's Road | 122 | 15. | Some Historic Squares ... | 157 |
| 13. | Queen Square ... ... | 135 | 16. | Along the Banks of the Frome | 167 |


# Plates


28. Queen's Road
29. Portrait of Charles Wells
30. Bristol Pageant
31. College Green
32. College Green
33. Queen's Road
34. Prince's Theatre
35. Queen's Road
36. Bristol Grammer School
37. Triangle Cinema
38. Coliseum
39. Queen's Road
40. Great George Street
41. Victoria Rooms
42. Whiteladies Road

43. Whiteladies Road
44. Queen Square
45. Queen Square
46. Merchants' Arms
47. Marsh Street
48. King Street
49. Prince Street
50. Prince Street
51. Prince Street
52. Dowry Square
53. Brunswick Square
54. Broad Weir
55. The Drawbridge
56. St. Augustine's Bridge
57. (Back Cover) Park Street
58. (Back Cover) College Green


(28) **Front Cover: 1905-1910:** The Art Gallery of 1905; the Drill Hall and Blind Asylum, demolished to make way for the University Tower, designed by Sir George Oatley and opened by King George V in 1925; off right, the future site of the Coliseum, a popular exhibition and dance hall, and silent cinema. Horse trough and fountain are now replaced by traffic signals, one-way signs, and double yellow lines. (See page 126).

**Back Cover: (57)** see page 122;
      **(58)** see page 102.

# Preface

"If I were a man of leisure, I might be tempted to write another Bristol book" wrote Charles Wells over 50 years ago. Reece Winstone, whose previous publications about our ancient City of Bristol have proved so popular, has done even better than Wells could have hoped. For now he has revived and revised the story of Bristol's old streets and old buildings which Charles Wells recorded in his column "Written in a Library" in the old "Bristol Times and Mirror".

As with some other provincial papers, the "Times and Mirror" had no nominal editor, but Charles Wells was *de facto* editor of the paper and his literary contributions to it commanded great respect. Although a native of Lincolnshire, his knowledge of our City was unrivalled.

The old files of the "Times and Mirror" are still available at the Bristol Central Library to those who have the time and patience to dig them out and peruse them. But here in a pocket-sized book, Reece Winstone has opened the storehouse of Wells's memory and in addition, has enabled his readers to see through the eyes of Wells, the Bristol that has now virtually disappeared. Some historical old buildings still remain, and these are carefully preserved, but the Bristol that Charles Wells knew so well has gone for ever. Many streets and their names have disappeared completely. The war and replanning have changed the face of our City so that Wells today would feel a stranger.

What was a valuable record in 1924 is a fascinating story today of the Bristol which many of the younger generation never knew, and many of the older generation may well have forgotten. I sincerely hope that this new publication will receive the support which it deserves. Its interest and value will grow with the years.

Walter A. Hawkins

# The Career of Charles Wells

Charles Wells was born at Lough, Lincs, in 1859; in 1881 he joined the staff of the "Bath Chronicle" and in 1886 became the chief reporter of the "Bristol Times and Mirror"; he was made a director of that newspaper in 1919. He died on 26th September 1932, after 55 years a journalist, 46 with his Bristol paper.

Twice President of the Bristol and West of England Press Fund, he was honoured by the Institute of Journalists in the same manner. He was a Governor of Queen Elizabeth's Hospital, and President of the following:—

> Bristol and Gloucestershire Archaeological Society.
> Bristol Society of Antiquaries.
> Bristol Kyrle (now Civic) Society.
> Bristol Commercial Rooms.
> Bristol Rotary Club (and several others).

The auther of "Historic Bristol", and "A Short History of the Port of Bristol", he was joint editor of "Bristol and the Grear War".

# Archie Powell's Tribute

"Mr. Charles Wells was a man of many parts, and loyally supported all good causes in Bristol. He became actively identified with numerous institutions and societies, whose interests he served with pen and voice. A great reader as well as writer, he acquired by years of patient research, a wonderful store of historic information of which citizens received full benefit by his writings and lectures. Older Bristolians have marvelled at Mr. Wells's apparently inexhaustive local knowledge, and many who appreciated his contributions to books and newspapers will rank him with such notable local historians as John Taylor, and John Latimer."

### PLEASE NOTE

**It should be emphasized that Charles Wells was writing about the Bristol of 1924; the Editor's footnotes bring this up to date to 1975.**

# Editor's Instruction to Volume Two

My first appreciation of the history of my native city was in 1922, when I saved my first newspaper cuttings:  these were sketches by F. G. Lewin illustrating descriptions of Bristol by Charles Wells.  I read and re-read the articles many times;  yellowed by age, they are still available for reference.  Recently some of the newspaper cuttings saved by the late Archie Powell came into my possession, including the work of Charles Wells, dated 1924.  As I read his essays, the thought came "Is it not possible to publish these in book form"?  It seemed worthwhile to make them available for other students of Bristol History;  the addition of footnotes would bring the story up to date.

The copyright of work by Charles Wells, published in his newspaper, "The Bristol Times and Mirror", passed to the Bristol United Press, publishers of the "Evening Post" and "Western Daily Press", and their Chairman readily gave permission for re-publication in book form.  Furthermore, Mr. Hawkins generously offered to contribute the Preface.

Another pleasant task was to choose the photographs to illustrate "the Bristol Charles Wells knew".  They came from my own collection, or by my own photography, or were kindly made available by the following:—Bristol Art Gallery, Bristol Central Library, Messrs. E. R. Keen and L. R. Reeves.  Thanks are expressed for technical assistance to Mrs. P. Manning, R. J. Acford Ltd. and The Bristol and West Engraving Co.  I am also very grateful to Miss Agnes Heath who kindly loaned the pleasant portrait of her brother-in-law, reproduced in plate 29.

Readers will note the page and plate numbers in this Volume Two run serially from Volume One.

If readers enjoy this book, and would like more of the writings of Charles Wells, please let me know.

Reece  Winstone

Chapter 11

# COLLEGE GREEN

Plates 31, 32 and 58


Delightful College Green is, as everybody knows, within the Cathedral precincts and takes its name from that fact, attendance at the Cathedral in old times being often spoken of as going to the "Colledge." If William Wyrcestre's measurements may be trusted the sanctuary area was coterminous[1] with that of The Green.

The Green has gradually developed from the times when it was a preaching place, a sanctuary, a burial place, an unfenced cattle-grazing ground, a ropery, a dress parade ground, a drill ground, till it is what we see it today, a charming spot for orderly recreation surrounded by historic churches, hotels and some of the most attractive shops that are to be found in Bristol. In its centre stands the replica of the ancient Civic Cross[2], and at one corner Boehm's marble statue of Queen Victoria erected by the citizens to celebrate her Majesty's jubilee. On the side opposite the Cathedral the properties have been purchased by the Corporation as a site for new municipal buildings when the right time comes—if it ever does[3]—to put them there. Once upon a time a little revenue was made out of the green by letting a rope-maker have a walk from east to west; and indirect profits were made by rights of burial and pasture. There are records of disputes

---

[1] Coterminous, an unusual word, meaning bordering.
[2] This Cross was cast out, with the tall trees, when the Green was lowered in 1950, so as "to improve the view of the Council House"!
[3] The time did indeed come, and building ensued from 1935–1955.

between the brethren of St. Augustine's and of St. Mark's over these matters. The Bishop of Worcester decided, in the time of Abbot Long, that the Canons were to bury their dead in the Green provided they kept the surface level, but neither party was to allow cattle to graze there. The Abbot could cut the grass to strew the floors of his two churches—the cathedral, and the Church of St. Augustine-the-Less.

This is how Evans records the matter in his Chronological History under date 1259: "A dispute between the monks of St. Augustine and the brethren of St. Mark about the right of burial in College Green, then the common cemetery of the Monastery. The Bishop of Worcester awarded to the brethren the liberty of burying before their house, but on condition of leaving the ground always level, because of the pleasantness of the place." But difficulties seem to have arisen again much later, for in 1322 Evans states that Peace in the Monastery was restored, and the dispute with the brethren of St. Mark's, about the cemetery, settled.

In 1495, according to the same historian, "The Sanctuary of St. Mary of St. Augustine's Green was broken," which is taken to mean that the elder Lady Chapel was no longer a sanctuary for the town's folk who were guilty of treason, all traitors being pronounced by Pope Alexander enemies to the Christian faith. In this year, too, "the King and Queen lodged at St. Augustine's Monastery."

John Latimer summarises the answers given to interrogatories on the occasion of the visitation of the diocese held in the Cathedral by Archbishop Laud on 31st May 1634. The first replies about the Cathedral and its services were described in the State Papers as "dark answers," and when the authorities complied with the pressure for more particulars "many discreditable truths came to light," says Latimer. The Dean and the Prebendaries all held other preferments and regarded four weeks' residence a year at Bristol Cathedral as sufficient. They sweated the other members of the staff, and the schoolmaster was too old and too fully occupied as Bishop's chaplain to train the boys for the choir. The prebendaries' houses were let to lay folk, and the library converted into a private dwelling. The school house in the Green was used as a tennis court, and the cathedral was used as a common passage to the palace and other houses in the cloisters. College Green was in a scandalous condition, being ploughed up by the sledges carrying clothes to dry on Brandon Hill, while the Corporation had erected a whipping-post in the centre for castigating offenders, and a rout of disorderly people played stop-ball and other games from morning to night, on Sundays as well as on week-days. In February 1638, peremptory instructions to reform matters were given by the Archbishop, but the Dean and Chapter resisted for nearly two years before obeying.

According to Latimer again, the Corporation in June 1709 gave £40 to the fund raised by the Dean and Chapter and the inhabitants of the Green towards fencing and improving it. Trees were planted in a double row—to replace old ones, most of which had been blown down by the great storm of November 1703, when the north transept window of the Cathedral was smashed to pieces. Still the Green continued to be neglected by the Dean and Chapter, and in 1756 the Corporation in response to a memorial from the inhabitants, voted 40 guineas for restoration of the turf and paths. Thereupon the capitular body felt compelled to add 15 guineas. There was some bickering between the Dean and Chapter over the improvement scheme, which included the removal of the Cross and the cutting off of a small part of the Green. The Dean objected, not on the merits of the proposal, but because he nearly always objected to what the Prebendaries proposed. He repented just a few days before he died!

The Dean and Chapter granted the inhabitants of the Green leave, in March 1790, to put up a watch-box in the middle "for their safety and protection" from the footpads and burglars who had been a pest for several years. To assist in this work in the city generally able-bodied young men of good character were employed as night patrols.

The entrance from St. Augustine's Parade, then called St. Augustine's Back, was up to the end of 1736 so dark, narrow, and steep that the growing traffic caused much congestion, and the Corporation spent £359 on reducing the gradient, leaving the widening to be done much later and by instalments. The first widening took place in 1775-6 under the provisions of the Improvement Act of 1766, when some old houses standing on The Butts were also removed.[4] The Corporation, the Society

---

(4) Now Canon's Road.

of Merchant Venturers, and the inhabitants divided the cots of the widening, which was £2,400. Within the last forty years there have been further widenings by taking slices off the churchyard of St. Augustine-the-Less, and there is now a fine broad approach to the Green from the centre of the city. All human remains disturbed were re-interred in Arno's Vale Cemetery.

From the Gaunts' Pipe which supplied water to Queen Elizabeth's Hospital (the City School) and neighbouring houses in College Green, it was a quite ordinary thing at intervals to remove the bodies of cats and other dead animals! Towards the end of the seventeenth century a supply was made available to some of the Corporation tenants in the Green from Jacob's Wells, but it proved inadequate, and a cistern was built near the old Gaunt's Hospital, from which pipes conducted water to the houses. Afterwards this cistern or reservoir was re-built on a larger scale, and I believe it still exists in the premises at the corner of College Green and Unity Street, though of course the Water Works Company now supply all the houses and shops.

Up to the sixteenth century College Green and neighbourhood had few buildings beyond those connected with the Cathedral, and the whole area was largely pasture and gardens. The Green was sometimes used as a parade ground for the trained bands, and commonly as a playground. It was being used as a volunteer parade ground as late as the nineteenth century. The Masonry was an enclosed space between the two churches dedicated to St. Augustine, and this for revenue purposes was let for building, but early in the eighteenth century the houses nearest the Cathedral were pulled down and an approach to Trinity Street was laid out. Trinity Street covers the site of a monastic garden.

At the west end of the Cathedral was what was known as the Minister House,[5] where in 1758 Mary Robinson ("Perdita") was born. She has stated that the deep tones of the organ and the chanting of the choir were audible in her nursery, and she remembered with what pleasure she listened to the music in childhood. The house became a ruin and has long since been demolished, but there is a drawing of it in Skelton's "Antiquities of Bristol".

---

[5] This is usually described as Minster House (see Latimer). The venerable building is illustrated in "1879–1874", plate 43; and "1874–1866", plates 55, 56.

Building around the Green must have proceeded pretty rapidly in the eighteenth century. Some dignified examples survive. Matthews's Directory, 1793–4, gives the addresses of several of the Cathedral and other clergy in College Green, Lower Green or College Street, but the Bishop (Dr. Spencer Madan) "resides partly at London and partly at Bristol Palace"; and Dr. John Hallam, the Dean (grandfather of Tennyson's friend), "half the year at Windsor, and half a year at Bristol Deanery." Dr. G. M. Johnson and Mr. J. P. Noble, surgeon, lived in the Green. There also, at No. 20, dwelt Isaace Amos, gentleman. John Barrow, merchant, was at No. 17; Granfield Becher (No. 12); Thomas Blagden, gentleman; Mrs. Mary Bowen (No. 18); Samuel Brooks, Custom House Officer; Lettice Brown, lodging-house keeper (No. 5); Captains Samuel and George Cooper (No. 23); Sir John Durbin, Kt.; William Henep, glazier; Miss Home, Ladies' Boarding School; Sir James Larouche, Bt.; Mosely Latham, newsman (No. 6); James M'Taggart, merchant (No. 14); William Parsons, merchant (No. 7); Charles Partridge (No. 3); John Powell, Collector of the Customs; Edmund Prichard, deal merchant; Freeman Smith, Sword Bearer; —Studley, merchant; Robert Walker, dancing master; Wasbrough and Son, organists; and Samuel Worrall, Town Clerk, are other names of late eighteenth-century residents of College Green. While staying at No. 26, College Green in May 1802 Dr. Jenner sent a letter to Felix Farley's Bristol Journal saying: "So many accidents having happened in Vaccine Inoculation within the City of Bristol, which have been mentioned by way of reproach, Mr. Jenner thinks it justice to himself and the cause to assert that such accidents attach only to the improper management of the inoculation."

If one looks over the Deanery Road Bridge[6] on the left one may see an old house with a tablet on the front stating that Samuel Taylor Coleridge lived there—No. 48, College Street.[7] That was in 1794, when Coleridge and his young friends Robert Southey, Robert Lovell and George Burnett were lodging in the house considering their plans for sailing to America and founding a social colony on the banks of the

---

[6] It is no longer a bridge—College Street (which it first spanned in c. 1870) was demolished 1955–1958.

[7] The Coleridge house is illustrated in "1950–1953", plate 30.

Susquehannah, where everything was to be in common in a State to be called Pantisocracy. Human perfectibility was to be the aim. "We freight a ship, carrying out with us ploughs and other implements of husbandry," exclaimed the enthusiastic Lovell to the cautious Cottle. Soon afterwards there came this note to Cottle:

"My dear Sir,—
"Can you conveniently lend me five pounds, as we want a little more than four pounds to make up our lodging bill, which is indeed much higher than we expected; seven weeks, and Burnett's lodging for twelve weeks amounting to eleven pounds.

"Yours affectionately,<br>"S. T. Coleridge."

Cottle lent the money. "Never did I lend money with such unmingled pleasure, for now I ceased to be haunted day and night with the spectre of the ship! the ship! which was to effect such incalculable mischief." Southey was not quite so keen on Pantisocracy as was Coleridge and some of the others, but at the age of 21 we are all venturesome, and he was that age when he wrote to his brother Tom, then a midshipman in the Navy, "In March we depart for America. Lovell, his wife, brother, and two of his sisters; all the Frickers; my mother, Miss Peggy, and brothers; Heath, apothecary, etc.; G. Burnett, S. T. Coleridge, Robert Allen, and Robert Southey." His mother said he was mad; "if so," the letter continued, "she is bit by me, for she wishes to go as much as I do." His aunt knew nothing about it, and Southey rightly thought that it would "surprise her, but not very agreeably." When she did learn of the scheme and of her nephew's engagement to marry one of the Fricker girls, she "let go" at him with some startling effect. "Here's a row! here's a kick up! here's a pretty commence!" said he in his next letter to his brother Tom, written in Bath on October 19, 1794. "We have had a revolution in the College Green, and I have been turned out of doors in a wet night. Lo and behold, even like mine own brother, I was penniless: it was late in the evening; the wind blew and the rain fell, and I had walked from Bath in the morning. Luckily my father's old great coat was at Lovell's. I clapt it on, swallowed a glass of brandy, and set off; I met an old drunken man three miles off, and was obliged to drag him all the way to Bath, nine miles! Oh, Patience, Patience, thou hast often helped poor Robert Southey, but never didst thou stand him in more need than on Friday, the 17th of October 1794. Well, Tom, here I am. My aunt has declared she will never see my face again, or open a letter of my writing—So be it. I do my duty, and will continue to do it, be the consequences what they may. You are unpleasantly situated, so is my mother, so were we all till this grand scheme of Pantisocracy flashed upon our minds, and now all is perfectly delightful. . . . My aunt abuses poor Lovell most unmercifully, and attributes the whole scheme to him; you know it was concerted between Burnett and me. But of all the whole catalogues of enormities, nothing enrages my aunt so much as my intended marriage with Mrs. Lovell's sister, Edith; this will hardly take place till we arrive in America; it rouses all the whole army of prejudices in my aunt's breast. Pride leads the fiery host, and a pretty kick up they must make there." Pantisocracy died a natural death. Southey married his Edith; but he was never forgiven by Aunt Tyler, and he never saw her again.

It should be impossible for any Bristolian to stroll in College Green without feeling that he is on historic ground. So no doubt felt the author of "The New Bristol Guide," which appeared in 1847. He describes it as "a little poetic jeu d'espirit,' composed "during an idle week" to amuse himself, and it contains lines descriptive of a walk through the antient city with Madame Bristowa, in the course of which the pair come

> To College Green, that central station,
>     Where the Cathedral towers, and taught me
> A little of its antient history,
>     Which mingles with masonic mystery.
> "See," said the eloquent dame,
>     "This old Cathedral tower
> Stands on a spot of fame."
>     "I've seen," said she, "the hour
> When this same College Green
>     Form'd a low rocky hill,
> On which the antique Britons, keen
>     Of eye and hand, did worship still
> Beneath one mighty old oak tree,
>     Symbol to them of Diety."

And Madam proceeds to tell of Druid priest seizing a golden knife to cut the mistletoe—

> . . . and then, in token
>    Of the great sacrifice, he slew
> Two milk-white bulls; and peace was spoken;
>    While as the bards their song renew.
> There the Romans invoked great Mars to quell their
> foe.
> And there, too, have I seen the crowd
>    Of Saxons worship, and fill high
> Their yellow mead, to Odin vow'd,
>    And all Valhalla's chivalry.
> There, too, I saw, in the first age
>    Of the new Christian Church, a man
> Who preach'd of Christ.  The sainted sage
>    Stood in the midst of the wild clan
> Of Britons, Saxons, Celts; and, by
>    The power of his great ministry,
> Gain'd rapt attention to heaven's truth
>    From hoary eld and fiery youth.

The preacher is, of course, St. Augustine, and until Bishop Browne exploded the case by his historical research it had been firmly believed by generations that St. Augustine preached on College Green.  At first the promoters of the Bristol Pageant, following the lead of an earlier scheme of pageantry which never matured, proposed to represent this preaching as a scene, but almost immediately changed it for the visit of the boy King, Henry III.

So much history has gathered around College Green in the eight centuries of its existence that a considerable book could be devoted to its records.  Pre-eminently its character is, of course, ecclesiastical, but it is also a most agreeable spot for recreation. In the eighteenth century, it was a fashionable residential quarter—some of the shops still suggest that when we look above the handsome plate-glass windows.  Now there are large hotels in the Green, and the busy shops[8] do a high-class trade especially in women's and men's wear, jewellery, and confectionery.  Since 1894 the Corporation have taken over the

---

[8] Many of these shops were blitzed:  See "1953–1956", plates 75, 161; and "1890's", plate 82.

care of the Green on lease at a peppercorn rent from the Dean and Chapter, and it is now very nicely kept.

Standing out prominently around the Green are its three churches—the Cathedral almost filling the south side, St. Augustine-the-Less on the left of the entrance from St. Augustine's Bridge, and St. Mark's on the eastern side.

The Cathedral was originally an Augustinian Abbey founded in 1142 by Robert Fitzhardinge, the progenitor of the Berkeley family. It was converted into a Cathedral in 1542, soon after the Dissolution, and the dedication was changed to the Holy and Undivided Trinity. The Norman Church consisted of a nave nearly as long as the present, a transept, and a choir of three bays with a square east end. The chief builder of the present east end was Abbot Knowle (1306–32). The first addition to this church was the Elder Lady Chapel, a beautiful early English structure. Abbot Newbury (1428–73) built the central tower. The nave was allowed to go into ruin and was so dangerous that it was taken down in accordance with a recommendation of the King's Commissioner made in 1539. This disposes of the nonsense about Cromwell demolishing the nave by his artillery on Brandon Hill, There was no nave to the Cathedral between the middle of the sixteenth century and the middle of the nineteenth. It was not until 1866 that Canon J. P. Norris, sub-dean, issued an appeal for funds to re-build the nave and it was not completed until 1877.[9] The Western towers were added in 1888. Thus, in Dean Elliot's time the Cathedral was completed at a cost of £56,000. Dean Pigou carried through several interior improvements, including the erection of the screen. The total expenditure on the Cathedral since 1850 must be about £120,000. The surviving portions of the early church include the Chapter House and Vestibule, the great gateway leading into College Square, and the gateway to the Abbot's Lodge.[10]

The first Bishop was Paul Bush (1542–54). The charter of the See is dated 4th June 1542, and directs that there shall be a dean, six canons, six minor canons (one to act as sacrist), one deacon, six lay clerks, one master of the choristers, two masters of the choristers, two masters of the Grammar School, four

---

[9] The strange appearance of the Cathedral in Canon Norris's day is seen in "1866–1860", plate 54.

[10] Present day views of the Cathedral appear in "TO-DAY" 4th Ed., plates 48–57, and "TRADITION", plates 89–98.

almsmen, on sub-sacrist, one porter, one butler, and two cooks. The cooks and the butler disappeared long ago. The diocese was carved out of Salisbury diocese and that of Worcester, and included the county of Dorset. Several Bristol parishes which had been in the diocese of Gloucester were included, and three which belonged to Bath and Wells. In 1836 Dorset was restored to Salisbury, and for economy's sake Bristol diocese was merged into Gloucester, Bedminster (including Redcliff) going back to Bath and Wells. In 1845 Bedminster was returned to the Bristol portion of the joint Diocese of Gloucester and Bristol. In 1897, after many years of struggle to raise the endowment, Bristol was again made a separate diocese. Dr. George Forrest Browne, Bishop of Stepney, came as first Bishop of the re-constituted See, and did a great work in setting up the necessary machinery. He retired in 1914, and was succeeded by the present Bishop, Dr. George Nickson, who had been Bishop of Jarrow from 1906. Bishop Browne is living in Kensington, still active as a preacher and a historical writer, although he was born as long ago as December 1833.

Many people living remember the nave-less Cathedral, of which there are pictures extant. For a long time up to the end of the "fifties," the congregations were but small, because there was so little room. The transepts and the aisles were shut off, and, says Latimer, "the only accommodation offered to persons who did not purchase the favour of the beadles consisted of narrow, unfurnished, unbacked benches," to which the Prince of Wales was relegated when he was travelling incognito in the autumn of 1856. When "The Church-Goer" (Mr. Joseph Leech)[11] went to service one Sunday morning eighty years ago he found that stalking up and down the aisle and giving significant looks and nods had no effect on the "little white-headed, ruddy faced man, in drab smalls and long-gaiters to match, and a black serge cloak." It was only when a significant move was made to his waistcoat pocket (in imitation of others who got a seat), that a pew door was opened for him to enable him to take his "full benefit of twelve penny worth of prayers." He contemplated chartering the Bishop's throne on another occasion if it were not too expensive.

It is not to be supposed that nothing was done to the structure

---

[11] An extract from "The Church-Goer" appears in "BRISTOL'S EARLIEST PHOTOGRAPHS", page 36.

of the Cathedral before the re-building of the nave. There was a re-opening in February 1840 after certain alterations and restoration in the choir—which was arranged to serve as nave and choir—followed five years later by the placing there of a cast-iron stove,[12] the "immense black vertical flue" of which was carried up through the beautiful groined roof. In 1860–61 the stalls and screens were removed, and the walls stripped of woodwork and whitewash, revealing so much beauty that the work was extended and the sedilia, which had been destroyed round about 1603 to make room for the great monument to Sir John Young[13] and his wife, were skilfully restored. The cost of the work done then was nearly £13,000, of which the Dean and Chapter found over £7,000, and the public over £5,000. In 1865 the central tower and its piers were found to need strengthening, and £6,000 was the estimated cost. Smaller alterations, not always improvements, were made in the structure in the first half of last century, but it was not until the restoration of the central tower (1865–6) was in progress that Canon Norris boldly issued his appeal for funds to build the nave. Work on the making of Deanery Road had brought to light foundations of a never-finished nave and north porch. It was, by the by, while on this work that a trefoiled Gothic parapet on each side of the steps leading into College Green opposite the High Cross was destroyed,[14] and the present ugly iron railing substituted. There was a generous response to the appeal. One of the most notable was Mr. W. K. Wait's offer to build the north porch. Later when the western towers were added, Mr. J. W. Dod subscribed £5,000 towards the cost. The completion of the nave and towers[15] was celebrated by a special musical service in the Cathedral on June 8th 1888, when some 3,000 persons were present.

This great work, which cost £83,000, was carried out in the reign of Dean Elliot. On his death, in 1891 (he had been dean since 1850), Dr. Pigou, Dean of Chichester, was appointed to the vacant post, and he succeeded in the course of seven years in raising nearly £20,000 for the further restoration of the central tower and the Elder Lady Chapel, and the reconstruction and

---

[12] Part of the heating arrangements is seen in "BRISTOL'S EARLIEST PHOTO-GRAPHS", plate 25.
[13] This is illustrated in "TRADITION", plates 91, 92.
[14] This handsome parapet is seen in "EARLIEST PHOTOGRAPHS", plate 22.
[15] This work is seen in progress in the "1880's", plates 69–71.

embellishment of the choir—which was, to the annoyance of some of the older members of the congregation, now exclusively reserved for the clergy, lay clerks, and cathedral officials—and exterior work. The reredos is a memorial of Bishop Ellicott's long occupation of the See, 1863–97, as Bishop of Gloucester and Bristol, and was put up in 1899; and the screen is a memorial of Mr. W. K. Wait.

At the present time Dean Burroughs is appealing to complete a fund of £20,000, spent or to be spent on new vestries and other necessary improvements and repairs. The donations include £6,000 from Sir George Wills, Bt., for the vestries—a memorial of his father, the late Mr. Henry Overton Wills. One recalls that in Dean Pigou's time Sir George's father made it possible to provide the present organ by giving a handsome sum of money. He it was whom all Bristol gratefully remembers as the founder of the University.

G. W. Manby, in his "Fugitive Sketches" (1802), surveys the Cathedral from Brandon Hill, and says the church "claims no inconsiderable share of attention, not only by its structure, but its history, having been so much the object of Cromwell's revenge, from whence his artillery mutilated this consecrated pile." Not content with desolating this sacred fabric, he stained it with a barbarity almost past the power of cruelty to invent. Dr. Howel was then Bishop of the diocese, whose palace they not only uncovered for the sake of its lead, but, disgraceful to humanity! unroofed the very room where his lady lay confined in childbed." Manby, like many another writer of history, evidently disliked Cromwell, and so repeated with gusto this pure fiction about the bombarding of the Cathedral from Brandon Hill.

In the Cathedral, as would be expected, are many monuments and tablets referring us to the distinguished dead, lay citizens, as well as bishops and clergy. A notable inscription is that written by Robert Southey for Bishop Butler's monument, which is a rare example of dignified eulogium in restrained but good English. Dr. Butler held the See from 1738 to 1750. There are a few others that are excellent in character, and one of them is the quite recent tribute to the life and work of Richard Hakluyt (1553–1616), of the "Navigations," who was for thirty years a Prebendary of the Cathedral.

Attached to the Cathedral is the school which the abbots

founded.[16] It may claim to be the oldest existing educational establishment in this city of ancient schools. Primarily it was for the education of choir boys, and they continue to be educated there, but many other boys are admitted.

The ruins of the Bishop's Palace to the south are worth inspection; it may be regarded as a memorial of the wreckage of the Reform Riots of 1831. Bishop Butler spent over £4,000 in making the palace habitable.

St. Augustine-the-Less[17] is a dedication which survives, although, as we have seen, Augustine-the-Great changed its dedication when it was made the seat of a Bishop three hundred and eighty-two years ago. This smaller foundation is mentioned in deeds dated 1235, and the present church goes back to about 1480. In its old stained glass are fragments of the arms of Abbots Newland and Elliott. The churchyard formerly and until recent years stretched over a large portion of what is now the roadway to and from the Green.

Well-known Bristolians have been identified with the church for many generations, and some of them are commemorated on the walls and in the churchyard. Edward Shiercliff, a printer and stationer in the eighteenth century and publisher of a Bristol guide in 1789—the first to be produced locally—was a parishioner, and there is a monument to him in the church which tells that he died in February 1798, was of an ancient Yorkshire family, and was not only possessed "in an eminent degree every social virtue," but was "versed in polite Literature" and "skilled in the Liberal arts, while his brilliant talents recommended general respect."

St. Mark's Church, now known as the Lord Mayor's Chapel, having been purchased by the Corporation with the Maurice de Gaunt Hospital estates after the Dissolution was the hospital chapel. It is mentioned as early as 1230. For about 150 years the Corporation allowed it to be used by French Protestant refugees (Huguenots), but in 1721 the Corporation resumed possession. There are some interesting examples of early English architecture remaining in the little church, and some

---

[16] The Cathedral School is seen in "TRADITION", plate 97, and "TO-DAY", 4th Ed., plate 52. The ruins of the Bishop's Palace were removed in 1963 for the new Cathedral School hall.

[17] St. Augustine's, demolished 1962, is illustrated in "1956–1959" plates 122, 192; "1879–1874" plate 44.

16th century glass. The roof is the original old English structure, and there are some fine old effigies, including what are believed to be those of the founders, Maurice de Gaunt and Robert de Gourney, in chain armour.

Two monuments adorn the Green. In the centre stands the Civic High Cross, and at the south-east corner the statue of Queen Victoria erected by public subscription to mark the jubilee of her Majesty's reign. It was unveiled by H.R.H. the late Duke of Clarence on a very showery day in July 1888 (25th)[18]. The Prince was made an Honorary Freeman, his name being the first placed on Bristol's list under the Honorary Freedom of Boroughs Act, 1885.

The cross is a replica of the one which stood at the cross roads at the top of High Street. The earliest cross there was erected in the thirteenth century, its successor in 1373. There it remained until 1733, when, after an interval of storage at the Guildhall it was re-erected in the middle of the Green. There it was voted an obstruction in the way to and from the cathedral, and was taken down and removed in pieces to the Cloisters. A paragraph in Felix Farley's Bristol Journal of August 21 1762, states that "several workmen were employed raising the walks in College Green and in taking down the High Cross." This was precedent to the giving away of the cross by the next Dean (Dr. Cutts Barton), to his friend Mr. Henry Hoare, of Stourhead, two years later. The cross remains at Stourhead, where I saw it last summer in excellent preservation. It stands near one of the entrances to the grounds and can be well seen from the highway.[19]

At a meeting held on September 22 1848, the Dean of Bristol (Dr. Lamb) in the chair, it was decided to raise £650, the estimated cost of a replica of the original High Cross "of which," says Latimer, "the city was scandulously deprived by a Dean and Chapter of the last century." The Mayor (Mr. J. K. Haberfield) laid the foundation stone on August 8 1850, in the presence of a body of Freemasons and other citizens, and the cross was completed in November of the following year, but the £480 for the eight statues was not forthcoming, and the niches

---

remained empty until 1855, when the Freemasons inserted that of Edward III., the King whose charter instituted the town a county.[20] The effigies are as follows:—

King John, Henry III., Edward III., Edward IV., Henry VI., Elizabeth, James I., and Charles I.[21]

Three memorable crimes are associated with College Green, and I will summarise them for the benefit of those of my readers who are interested in criminology. Only one actually took place in the Green, but the association will be seen. On the site now occupied by the Royal Hotel (erected in 1868) stood No. 2, known as the "Great House." This was the residence of Mr. Jarrit Smith, a lawyer who on the death of his brother-in-law, Sir John Smyth in 1741, succeeded to Ashton Court, and in 1763 was made a baronet. He represented Bristol in Parliament from 1756 for twelve years. He had a very lucrative business as a lawyer and had a claim against his brother-in-law's estate of £20,000 or £30,000, and took the house and park and contents in satisfaction, his wife also inheriting a third share of the residue of the Ashton Court estate. He died in 1783, aged 91, and was buried with his parents at St. Mary, Redcliff.

One of his clients was Sir John Dineley (Goodere) Bt., and it was at the sinister suggestion of his brother Captain Goodere, R.N., of H.M.S. Ruby, then stationed in King Road, that Sir Dineley was invited by Mr. Smith to meet him at the Great House with a view to the amicable ending of a long-standing feud. Sir John had changed his name on succeeding to a maternal estate. He sometimes behaved like an insane man, and the "last straw" so far as the captain was concerned was the Baronet's act of cutting off the entail to family estates to which, in the case of the Baronet's prior death, the captain would have succeeded. Nursing his grievance until he became inflexibly murderous in his intentions, the captain engaged some of the choicest villains among his crew, and in the crew of a

---

[20] The Victorian Cross is seen without the first statue in "EARLIEST PHOTO-GRAPHS", plate 61; and seen with the statue of Edward III in "1866–1860", plate 13. The sad story of the further desecration in 1950 is recorded in "TO-DAY" 4th Ed., plates 82, 83—surely this was a treachery against the Crown, because the whole purpose of the two High Crosses was to express thanks to those monarchs who had given charters to Bristol, and thereby afforded citizens the opportunity to prosper by expanding the old town.

[21] The other seven statues (carved by Harry Hems) were set up in 1888. See the "1880's", plate 4.

privateer, and deliberately planned the capture and disposal
of his brother, Mr. Jarrit Smith, as requested, innocently
arranged the meeting of the brothers at his house for reconcili-
ation. The brothers met on 19th January 1741, and drank a
toast "to love and friendship" and then left.

Nearly opposite the Great House was a tavern, the White
Hart, whence the gang of ruffians sallied on a signal being
given, seized the Baronet, and in spite of his loud cries of
"Murder! I am Sir John Dineley," they carried him to the
Ruby's barge at Mardyke, and rowing to Kingroad, locked him
up in a cabin aboard the ship. The work of Press Gangs was
then too familiar in Bristol to excite much notice; the rule of
chance spectators being to keep themselves out of danger. All
this was done according to plan under Captain Goodere's
direction and in his presence, the captain keeping the officers
and decent men of his ship at bay with his sword and telling
them that the victim was a madman. During the night Sir John
was strangled by Mahony and White with a piece of rope, the
captain dividing the money found on the body among the
blackguards who had followed instructions.

Sir Michael Foster was Recorder of Bristol at the time, and
when the Admiralty, seeing that the murder was alleged to have
been committed in Kingroad, asked them by what authority the
case was proposed to be tried in Bristol, the Recorder replied at
considerable length, saying that jurisdiction was claimed "as
the place is within the body of the county of the city of Bristol,
which we ground on charter and usage." Edward III. had
made Bristol a county, and the consequent perambulation of
the boundaries in September '47 Edward III.[22] set forth the
limits by water and land. Parliament confirmed the boundaries,
as did subsequent charters. H.M.S. Ruby lay within the limits
of the county "and, indeed no ship can, as I am informed by a
very skilful mariner, an officer of the port, lie in Kingroad
unless it lies near a mile within our eastern and northern
limits. In fact Kingroad hath been always esteemed part of the
county of Bristol. The city water-bailiffs and other officers have
executed processes of all kinds there; and all offences committed there have been tried and determined either at our

---

[22] This is the old style of reckoning to indicate the 47th year of the reign of
Edward III.

quarter sessions or gaol delivery as the nature of the case demanded." The Attorney-General replied that he and the Solicitor-General were fully satisfied, and the Admiralty had no thought of injuring Bristol's jurisdiction.

Next day some of the crew, satisfied that a cold-blooded murder had been done, mutinied and placed their captain under arrest. After no little hesitation the Mayor sent the Water Bailiff to fetch him. Mahony and White were afterwards arrested. The captain protested his innocence, and insisted and was allowed to walk through the streets to gaol wearing the red cloak of his station in society. An attempt at his rescue failed, and in the end all three malefactors admitted their guilt and were hanged on St. Michael's Hill, April 15th, together with a woman who had murdered her baby. Mahony's body was exhibited at the Royal Infirmary to the students as an object lesson in anatomy, and was afterwards hung in chains on Dunball Island, "in the parish of St. Stephen's," as the Mayor's order described it. Captain Goodere's body was given to his friends, who buried it in the family vault in Herefordshire. This murder is become a "classic crime", and has been responsible for the publication not only of the usual kind of now old-fashioned chap book, but of serious essays in criminology by students of some eminence.

This letter from Lady Dineley, who was a daughter of Alderman John Lawford, of Bristol, dated 1741, relates to the murder, and shows how a member of Society would spell in that day. I had written of the spelling that it was "free and easy," but it is not easy to read in the present day:—

"Dr Cosen. Whatt your hard in the new (news) of poor Sr Jon is to trow and it have all mostt ben my Deth for I am fritt outt of my wits. So horrid a murder I never hard of, I can nott till you how but refure you to the newspaper which is very il rit. I have a greatt deall to say but my Hartt is to full. Dr Miss Chubb I must still be trublesume to you, to by me moung (mourning) I wood have itt in the very pink of ye mode and very sollom weed of Silk as is made on this a Kaous (occasions) and everything as be Long to a Wedw butt no Shou or Stokin that I have here.

I have sent my seys (size) but let itt be to big and Long that it may be alltudd. I have a blak nightt goond and Dr. cosn pray let itt be sentt the beginn of next week for Mr. Smith when I am obligd to be in Wostershere the Latta Inn of the week in great bisniss."

This widow afterwards married William Rayner, a printer, and died in 1757 at Stapleton, says Mr. W. J. Pountney, who lately copied this letter for Alderman Sheppard.

Sept. 27 1764, Mrs Frances Ruscombe and Mary Sweet, her servant, were found murdered in her house in College Green; which must have been done between one and two o'clock in the afternoon. The Corporation offered a reward of £100 and Mr. Nugent, M.P., £500 for the discovery of the perpetrator, but without effect, says a diarist.

This crime was discovered by a woman relative of Mrs. Ruscombe who had come to dine with her by invitation. On entering the house she was horrified to see Mrs. Ruscombe's body on the stairs, with her head mutilated. The servant's body was found in the back parlour with her head nearly severed. Both bodies were still warm. Robbery was the motive, a bag and a purse containing about £90 in gold being taken. Mr. Ruscombe, the husband, and Mrs. Ruscombe's sisters offered rewards of £10 and £52 10s. respectively. Several arrests were made, and among those detained was a baker named Peaceable Robert Matthews, who in 1748 was fined £6 12s. 6d. for selling short weight bread, the prosecutors being the Bakers' Company. They were perhaps made zealous for righteousness by the fact that they received part of the fines. Matthews was strongly suspected of this murder and robbery, but there was no proof discoverable against anybody. The case is mentioned by De Quincey (who learnt the details in one of his visits to Bristol) in "Murder as a Fine Art."

The house in which the crime was committed was afterwards pulled down and another built on the site by Sir Jarrit Smyth, who before he became the owner of Ashton Court and secured a title spelt his name Smith. On adopting the "y" which had been so common and still is, neither he nor any of the others pronounced the name with the long vowel sound.[23]

At Bristol Spring Assizes 1835—the first to be held by Sir Charles Wetherell, Recorder, since the riots of 1831—Mrs. Mary Ann Burdock, aged 34, was indicted for the murder of

---

[23] The last member of the Smyth family of Ashton Court was Dame Emily, who died in 1946.

Mrs. Clara Ann Smith, an elderly woman of means, who lodged with her at No. 17, Trinity Street, off the Green. The relatives of the deceased hearing nothing of her for over a year, made inquiries, and being dissatisfied with Mrs. Burdock's account of the death, obtained an order for the disinterment of the body, when it was found that the stomach contained sufficient arsenic to result in death. Mrs. Burdock had been feeding the deceased and had cautioned a servant not to eat any food that was left. The victim had received £800 shortly before her death, and Mrs. Burdock had suddenly become affluent. The trial lasted two days, and although the evidence was all circumstantial Mrs. Burdock was found guilty and sentenced to death. She maintained a callous demeanour, ordered her coffin—which was not to cost over £2—to be placed by her bed on her last night; was duly executed at the gaol in Cumberland Road on April 15th before a crowd of spectators estimated to number 50,000.

Full reports of the trial were published and are extant. There are also in pamphlet form two sermons preached on the crime by the Rev. T. F. Jennings, the gaol chaplain; one at St. Thomas's Church, where the preacher was curate, and one at St. Werburgh's, where he was evening lecturer. An illustrated broadside describes the execution, which took place at 12 noon. "Every place," it is said, "which commanded a view of the drop was crowded by an immense multitude of anxious spectators (as was also the Guildhall during the whole of the Trial crowded to excess) no Execution having taken place in this City for many years which has created such excitement, and it being 33 Years since the Execution of the two women for the Murder of one of their children on Pile Hill." There are some doggerel verses of warning to others. One reads:

> Now both young and old a warning take
>     Nee'er murder for your gain.
> For if you do, Mrs. Burdock's fate
>     Must repay you for your pains.

No doubt somebody put the verses to a poor chanting tune, and sang them in the streets to sell the broadside, as was done in much later cases—that of Constance Kent, for example.

A stone was placed over the victim's grave in the churchyard of St. Augustine-the-Less with this inscription: "Here lie the

remains of Clara Ann Smith, who was poisoned by Mary Ann
Burdock on October 26th 1833, who was executed for the same
in this city the 15th April 1835."[24]

Chapter 12

# PARK STREET & QUEEN'S ROAD

Plates 28, 33, 34, 35, 36, 37, 38, 39, 40, 41, 42, 43 and 57

Park Street, so named because it is made out of part of what was formerly known as Bullock's Park, is now one of our chief shopping streets, and one of our steepest, but by no means one of the oldest in the city. It was on August 9th 1740 that, as Latimer records, the Corporation granted to Alderman Nathanial Day for £20 per annum the reversion of a piece of land near the Boar's Head Inn, his purpose being to "open a street forty feet wide in Bullock's Park to lead from College Green up into the road toward Jacob's Well." Latimer quotes this as another instance of the deliberate movements of the time. Not a house was erected in Park Street till more than twenty years later, and there were some still to be built at the beginning of the nineteenth century.[1] Alderman Day had been chosen Sheriff in 1724, and Mayor thirteen years later. He was a member of the Corporation for 45 years up to his death in 1765.

John Evans, under date 1759, writes: "The design of opening and building Park Street, with Great George Street and Charlotte Street, now began to be entertained. In 1596 Bullock's Park, alias Amery's Close, and the Grange, a part whereof was Tapley's Garden (the extent of which may be seen in Roque's plan of 1742) were leased from the 21st of December for one thousand years at 1d. per annum, £45 to the representatives of Nathanial Day, and 5s. per annum to the King, and now held by three several families (the Daubenys, the Deverells, and that of Woodward, Bishop of Cloyne), together with two pieces of freehold land adjoining each other (at the foot of Park Street, next to Frog Lane) originally bought of— Worth and of—Hart, for one thousand years from October 1 1661. This year (1759), Sept. 29, part of the Boar's Head Inn yard, freehold and another small piece next to it, were added by purchase from Arthur Hart, executor of W. Hart, for the remainder of one thousand years. The progress which we have traced of this speculation, through all the changes of public credit and consequent mutations of individual interest, has left on our minds the impression that the view from College Green would be fitly and justly terminated by a monument to the memory of the chief sufferer, inscribed with the venerated name of Francis Ward." I presume that this was Mr. Francis Ward, who was president of the Dolphin Society in 1789, and who died in 1797 at the comparatively early age of 53.

Sixteen years later Evans has this note: "The building of Park Street, in Bullock's Park, began. It was, we believe, at the completion of Park Street that the conduit at the south-east corner of Unity Street was erected, for the conveyance from the spring rising at the head of Park Street. Previously on the site of Reeve's Hotel, College Place, stood 'the Water-House.' " Reeve's Hotel is now the Hydro.[2] It was originally Alderman John Noble's private mansion. He was made Mayor in 1791.

Latimer shows that it was only eighteen years after the scheme first came to the notice of the Corporation that Alderman Day and George Tyndale, his partner in the project, submitted their plans, and suggested that if they had a fresh lease they would lay out a road from the top of the new street to White Ladies' Gate, where it would join the turnpike road from the city over St. Michael's Hill,[3] and so afford a new and easier route for the mail coaches and other vehicles travelling to Aust. A Bill had just been passed by Parliament sanctioning the extension of Bristol turnpikes and a new road from Frog-lane "through certain grounds (the site of Park Street) to a gate on the Aust Road called White Lady's Gate." It will be noticed that the gate was named after one White Lady, not more. The Corporation granted the request of Messrs. Day

---


(2) The hotel, with its Turkish Baths, is now known as Brunel House (Offices).
(3) The turnpike survives in the "1850's", plate 58.

and Tyndale, subject to their keeping Park Street in repair; but it was not until February 1761 that building sites were offered for tender; and it was in that year, too, that the Turnpike Trustees decided to proceed with the White Lady's improvement.

An interesting proposition was made to the Common Council at its meeting on July 4 1829, by the senior member, Mr. William Weare, whose family had been members of the Corporation since the middle of the previous century, and probably held the record for the number of times they had declined the mayoralty though readily filling the office of sheriff. This Mr. Weare who had declined the mayoralty in 1795, now proposed to pay into the city purse a sum of £10,000 on condition that the Corporation paid him £500 a year for life, and at his death a like annuity to Henry Weare should he survive the donor. The Council agreed to the proposition and a deed was executed which contained the donor's suggestion that immediately, or soon after his death, the £10,000 should be spent on the improvement of Redcliff and Baldwin Streets, the making of a new street from St. Augustine's Place to Trenchard Street, and the improvement of the streets at the lower end of Park Street. What happened was that the money was invested and in 1840 it was added under an Act of Parliament authorising building regulations and street improvements, to £15,000 borrowed for these purposes and so helped to form an Improvement Fund of £25,000. William Weare died in December 1836, aged 84 years. He was never an Alderman or Sheriff, but he served a year as warden of the Merchant Venturers.

The improvement of the bottom of Park Street did not come until 1871 when at a cost of £27,000 the gradient between College Green and the Philosophical Institution (now the Freemasons' Hall) was reduced by the construction of the bridge which constitutes what we call Park Street Viaduct.

It will amuse the present generation used to seeing motor vehicles and cycles race up the street to know that early in March 1856 we published particulars of a joint stock company, formed under the then new Limited Liability Act, whose revenue was to be earned by "raising passengers and goods from the low levels of some parts of Bristol to the more elevated portions of Clifton by machinery." But this was no new idea to the people of the time, for there had been several proposals to fix an engine at the top of Park Street for drawing up heavily-laden carts and waggons. The problem was ultimately solved for a generation or two by the making of Colston Street and Perry Road.

One of the first houses to be erected was No. 10. It was purchased, if not built to their order by the Misses Mary More and sisters, who had opened a school for young ladies at No. 6, Trinity Street, College Green, at Easter 1758. Hannah More was at this time a girl of twelve years and therefore did not found the school, though it is commonly believed that she did. The school was removed to No. 10, Park Street about 1762.

Hannah More was always more inclined to teach by her pen than otherwise, and in the autumn of 1789 the sisters all retired to Cowslip Green, being apparently very prosperous with their school. Miss Selina Mills, one of the staff, carried on assisted by her sisters. In 1799 she married Mr. Zachary Macauley and became the mother of Lord Macaulay. Among her pupils in 1791 was Miss Clementina Clerke, an heiress, aged 16, who ran away to Gretna Green with Richard Vining Perry, a surgeon, of Stokes Croft. Perry was put on his trial before the Recorder, Mr. Vicary Gibbs, in 1794, for abduction and marrying Miss Clerke against her consent and for the sake of her money. But the lady made it so plain in her evidence that she was a con-senting party and was perfectly happy as Mrs. Perry that the Recorder could only say the jury must return a verdict of "Not guilty." which they did. For some years until lately we preserved the name of Hannah More in Park Street by naming a room behind No. 45, Hannah More Hall.[4] It was used for public meetings, concerts, etc., but is now solely used for commerce.

The first notable building in Park Street to be erected early in the nineteenth century was the Bristol Philosophical and Literary Institution. A site was purchased at the foot of the hill on the left, and early in 1823 the building was opened, having cost £11,000. At the banquet to celebrate the event it is related that one of the most ardent promoters, Mr. Samuel Lunell, let an apple fall from his hand and asked the company why it fell rather than rose, concluding with the question,

---

"What keeps the moon up in the sky?" There was no other response than an alderman's irrelevant "Pass the decanter, please." That may be a story invented to show contempt for the scientific knowledge of the leading public men of Bristol in 1823. It would have been just as appropriately applied in any other town at that date; and I am not at all sure that at any public dinner or meeting to-day these questions about the apple and the moon[5] would be certain to receive a ready and correct answer, University men and women being absent. The passer-by, who is not a Freemason, and therefore must not enter the hall, may see in the exquisite alto-relievo frieze, wrought by Edward Hodges Baily, R.A., son of a Bristol ship's carver, something well worth notice, and not excelled by any internal decoration.[6]

For financial reasons the Institution and the old Bristol Library Society combined, and the Museum in Queen's Road was erected to house the contents of both Institution and Library, and so in 1871 the new building was opened as the Bristol Museum and Library, maintained by private subscription. The Freemasons of Bristol bought the Institution for £5,960 and converted it into their hall, which it is to this day. But want of funds still crippled the Museum and Library. About £14,000 had been spent on the incompleted building before occupation, and an appeal in 1873 for funds to complete it largely failed. In 1893 the Corporation agreed to take over the Museum and Library. Sir Charles Wathen, who was several times Mayor, undertaking to clear the debt of £2,871. Sir Charles died suddenly at a meeting of the Council in February 1894, before the transfer was carried through, but his widow and other relatives fulfilled the promise. The books went to the Central Library in College Green. They include works read by Coleridge and his friends while they lived in Bristol.

Thanks to the munificence of the late Lord Winterstoke (then Sir William Henry Wills, Bt.), an Art Gallery has been added— opened in 1905, having cost upwards of £40,000. A few years earlier the Corporation bought for £10,000 the Drill Hall and headquarters of the old Bristol Rifle Corps (now the 4th

---

Gloucesters), who have erected a much finer drill hall in Old Market Street.

One of the conditions laid down by the donor of the Art Gallery was that a certain sum should be spent annually on the purchase of works of art, and he suggested, but did not insist on, Sunday opening. The Art Gallery has attracted many valuable gifts and loans, and this is also true of the Museum,[7] so much so that there is urgent need for an extension on the site of the Drill Hall, which is at present no more than a store room. The whole of the product of the three-halfpenny rate is required for maintenance. What is wanted is that somebody should follow Lord Winterstoke's example and pay for the inclusion of the Drill Hall site in the scheme of buildings.[8]

A lease of an acre of land, part of Brandon Hill, was granted by the Corporation in December 1776 to Joseph Farrell, who was then building a house in Great George Street, off Park Street. Again, in December 1785, Lowbridge Bright, living in the same street, obtained a lease of part of the same hill. This appropriation of public property to private enjoyment seems, as Latimer remarks, to have excited no public remark, but the two leases may have referred to the same acre. I suppose Farrell's present-day successors in occupation are the Clergy Daughters' School. He was president of the Dolphin Society in 1753, and Lowbridge Bright, Governor of the Incorporation of the Poor, 1792–4. Some years ago Professor William Knight, the Wordsworthian, made the interesting discovery that Wordsworth and Coleridge first met at No. 7 Great George Street,[9] their host being John Pinney, father of the Mayor of Bristol, who was in office at the time of the Reform Riots in 1831.

St. George's Church is assumed to be in Great George Street, but those who care to avoid the imposing flight of steps leading to it may enter more easily from Charlotte Street. This is a church designed by Sir Robert Smirke, the architect of the Council House and is the last church to be erected in Bristol on

---

[7] Blitzed in 1940, the Museum's activities were moved to the Art Gallery, and so remain to this day, despite abortive and abandoned efforts to erect a new complex in Wine Street.

[8] The hope of Charles Wells was fulfilled a few years after he wrote the above.

[9] John Pinney's house became Georgian House in 1939, the first Georgian Museum in the country, through the generosity of the late Canon R. T. Cole. See "TO-DAY", 4th Ed., plates 87, 88.

a classical model.[10]  It was opened in 1823, and last year the centenary was appropriately observed.  It was built as a chapel-of-ease for St. Augustine-the-Less, in College Green, but gained its parochial independence in 1832.  At one period of his life Canon J. P. Norris was vicar, the man who, as Sub-Dean of the Cathedral, started the fund for re-building the Cathedral nave.

In 1786 a start was made with Berkeley Square to meet the demand of wealthy citizens who wished to live on the higher parts.[11]  But both Berkeley Square and Charlotte Street, which followed, "hung fire" for a long time, and as late as August 1799 several partly-built houses were offered for sale.

I am indebted to Mr. W. J. Pountney for these hitherto unpublished extracts from a private diary (William Dyer's):—

"1786, December 1.—Died, Richard Walker, who lived in Upper Maudlin Lane, but was formerly a linen draper in Mary-le-Port Street. . . . Owner of the field on which after his decease Berkeley Square and Crescent were built.  Mr. Strangeways, a clergyman, married his daughter, and settled on her the field, formerly a garden behind Berkeley Crescent.  Strangeways and Thomas Morgan, the Attorney, agreed with her trustees to pay them £60 a year (i.e. £30 each) for the purpose of building thereon, with a view to gain from ground-rents—a most ruinous undertaking."

"1791, September 10.—Heard that Thomas Tyndall sold the Fort House and Park at the price of £40,000, that £20,000 was paid him on account, and he took a mortgage for £20,000. . . . That it was intended to build a crescent in pursuance of their plan, dug out foundations and partly erected two or three houses, but after a while the chief part of these purchasers and enterprisers became bankrupt, when Mr. Tyndall sued for and obtained a decree of foreclosure, whereby the £20,000, together with the mortgaged premises, became his property; but after his decease said premises were exposed to sale at public auction, but no one bidding to the amount of £20,000 and interest due thereon, they were bought in by Tyndall and Son, and legally conveyed to him."

"1794, June 14.—Mr. George Miller bought two houses at

---

public auction (Nos. 1 and 2) in Berkeley Crescent for £1,160. These were then recently finished.”

1794, December 12.—Dyer's brother had lived in Mr. Miller's house, 1, Berkeley Crescent, after the brother left it. William Dyer, the writer of the diary, bought it.

“1796, January 26.—Mr. George Miller on observing my charges for agency, only £63 a year, remarked that it was too little, and that he shou'd make up the difference, and at length he generously gave me by way of compensation, the dwelling house, No. 2, in Berkeley Crescent.”

These were transferred to Dyer 24 and 25 March 1796. On September 28 of same year William Dyer writes: “The road repaired at the expense of St. Augustine's, under the management of Solomon Roach, from the bottom of the lane that passes by my side door, through the village, where is a public-house, with the sign of Berkeley Castle, to the foot of the hill leading to Belle View and to Clifton.”

This seems to show that Berkeley Place was then considered and called a village.

“1799, April 25.—The grounds round Mr. Tyndall's house were again laid out as a Gentleman's Garden. A new carriage road to the house was made in 1801.”

While Great George Street, Charlotte Street and Berkeley Square remain residential, the vast majority of Park Street houses have long ago been converted into shops,[12] and the one or two that have not undergone structural alterations are no longer exclusively private dwellings.

Matthews's Bristol Directory of 1793–4 shows that clergy, doctors, and merchants were then beginning to move up the hill into Park Street and neighbourhood.

On the summit of Brandon Hill there was once a hermitage, and the tradition says that the first occupant was a woman, Lucy de Newchurch. In the late 16th century there was a mill, and Mr. Walker, miller, of the Hill, was fined by the Corporation in 1573 for breaking the city pound and taking out his horse, which had been straying. The mill at this time was a new one of wood, and had been erected by the Town Clerk (William Rede), who in 1564 had obtained a sixty-years' lease on Brandon Hill, paying the Corporation a rent of £1 6s. 8d. In 1581

---

[12] The last building with steps to the front door is seen in “1953–1956”, plate 170.

the Crown startled the Corporation and the town by claiming Brandon Hill as its property. Some designing creature had discovered that a plot of ground on the top of the Hill which had been given to Tewkesbury Abbey by Robert, Earl of Gloucester, when he founded St. James's Priory, had been overlooked at the Dissolution probably because it yielded no rent. The discoverers obtained from Queen Elizabeth a grant of the ground as concealed Crown land. They then forced the Corporation to buy them out, selling their fee farm rent of 5s. for £50. Brandon Hill was a place for drying clothes from time immemorial, and that is formally admitted in a Corporation deed dated 1533, the year in which Elizabeth was born. Therefore, if as tradition has it, the Queen granted the washerwomen of Bristol this right, it was no original grant but merely a confirmation of an old right.[13]

When the city was defended in the time of the Civil War an important fort was that on Brandon Hill.

The guns on the Hill to-day are two 36-pounders captured from the Russians in the Crimea, and were placed there in August 1857.[14] Each gun is nine feet long and weighs three tons. They arrived on the 19th of the month and were welcomed by great crowds of citizens who lined the route through the principal streets. Access to the hill was obtained by knocking away a portion of the wall in Berkeley Square, and in addition to a team of eight horses everybody who could get near enough helped to rush the guns into position.

The main feature on the hill to-day is the Cabot Tower[15] erected by public subscription in 1897–8, to mark the fourth centenary of the discovery of North America by John Cabot. It is 105 feet high and cost £3,250. Citizens and visitors who are sufficiently active delight to climb up inside and get the magnificent views that are to be had from the balcony. Others are content to stay below, admire the grace and beauty of this memorial of a great Bristol event, and persuade themselves that after all the view from the natural summit is exceedingly fine. The tower is lit by electricity at night and so forms a conspicuous beacon for a radius of many miles. The hill is in the care of the Corporation and quite lately a welcome addition

---

[13] The sign on Brandon Hill is seen in "FASHION", plate 190.
[14] The Russian guns, illustrated in the "1880's", plate 128, went for munitions in the Hitler War.
[15] See "TO-DAY", 4th Ed., plate 81.

to its amenities has been made by the construction of a bowling green.

To a meeting of the Town Council in August 1845, the Improvement Committee presented a report which ultimately resulted in the making of Victoria Street (a new road from Bristol Bridge to Temple Meads railway station) and in other improvements, one of which was the improvement of the road from Park Street to the Victoria Rooms. Nothing was done with either of these proposals for many years until on the continuous pressure of the residents of Clifton the Council bought sufficient of Mr. Tyndall's land opposite his park, to secure a widening of the thoroughfare beyond Park Street, and in 1854 named it Queen's Road subsequently defining it as extending from Park Street to Victoria Square, which is the present extent. In the middle of 1859 the foundations were laid of the handsome ranges of buildings known as the Royal Promenade, now a fine series of shops; and in the autumn of 1864 the stables and coach-houses of Berkeley Square began to give way to a row of shops, some of which were let at a greater rent than the houses in the square commanded. They are to-day among the most attractive of the Queen's Road shops. Many years later Messrs. Lennard's, Ltd., made Bristol their headquarters and erected the imposing block of buildings opposite what was once the main entrance to Tyndall's Park when it was in private ownership.

Mr. Pountney sends me this interesting information:—"In Queen's Road where Newbury's shop now is[16] was a large quarry extending towards Berkeley Place. The foundations of this block of shops had to be made over 30 feet deep in consequence. Reed's house opposite the Church House (late Queen's Hotel),[17] was built in upper part of the quarry—notice its present level in comparison with the new road. The old road to Clifton went through this quarry. Gallows-Acre Lane commenced in those days opposite Tyndall's gates[18] where the new Richmond Hill joined what is now Queen's Road. When I was a

---

[16] This refers to Lennard's building, with Newbury & Spindler the furniture dealers in occupation: this spot after the bombing is well seen in "BLITZED", plate 149; Newbury's moved to modern showrooms in Park Street (the site of the Hannah More rooms already mentioned) but the business ended in 1971.

[17] Seen as a hotel in "1914–1900", plate 38; subsequently Gardiner's, Jones's, and J. F. Taylor's.

[18] The entrance to Tyndall's Park is seen in "EARLIEST PHOTOGRAPHS", plate 9.

boy Gallows-Acre Lane[19] commenced where Pembroke Road now starts. We used to pick blackberries there. The little road[20] by side of Queen's Road, as you go from Pembroke Road to Clifton, is part of the old Clifton Road."

Whenever you come upon a reference to Bishop's College, Bristol, where some notable citizens were educated, you should remember that it stood on the site now covered by the Art Gallery facing Queen's Road. Dr. Monk, who had been but recently appointed Bishop of Gloucester and Bristol, lent himself to a movement to found a "Bishop's College" in opposition to the existing "Bristol College" in Park Row (where Lord Justice Fry and Walter Bagehot were educated), because of its theology. The Bishop's College was started in a house in Bellevue, Clifton, but soon afterwards (in October 1841) transferred to new premises erected in Queen's Road—originally intended for the Red Maids, but found too costly—the Bishop purchasing the block for £9,750 from the Charity Trustees. Two or three months later Bristol College was closed down by this competition. In 1861 the Bishop's College[21] was also obliged to close for financial reasons, and the premises were purchased by the promoters of a Volunteers' Club. By April 1888 the Conservative Party had possession of the place as the Salisbury Club,[22] named after the Prime Minister of the day. The club lasted until 1896.

It has been a long struggle from the University College of 1876, started in a house in Park Row[23] (now the headquarters of the South Midland R.E., and formerly of Bristol College) to the full University, with extensive range of buildings in Tyndall's Park, which when completed will excel those of any university outside Oxford and Cambridge. Here, again, the Wills family have been the main supporters, their benefactions amounting to many hundreds of thousands of pounds. Others too have given generously, the Fry family in particular being good friends from the earliest days.

In close proximity are the Grammar School, a foundation of

(19) For a further description of the lane with the gallows at the top, see "ANN GREEN" pages 33 and 106.

(20) This became the garden of Buckingham Place.

(21) The College buildings are seen in the "1880's", plate 118.

(22) What happened to some of the stonework is recorded in "TRADITION", plates 202, 203.

(23) The house in which the University began is seen in the "1880's", plate 116 (demolished 1969).

the sixteenth century; the Baptist College, dating back to 1679; and the more modern Western College for the training of Congregational ministers. The Baptist College was in Stokes Croft[24] until a few years ago; and the Western College at Plymouth.

Undoubtedly the finest site in Clifton is that before the Victoria Rooms. These Rooms add much to the attractiveness of this space. They were erected in 1840–42[25] at a cost of £28,000, the promoters being prominent members of the Conservative Party. In July 1842 there was sufficient unbuilt space around the Rooms to permit of a meeting of the Royal Agricultural Society. Implements were exhibited on what is now the site of The Triangle, and in fields behind the Victoria Rooms were the cattle sheds.

The beautifully proportioned facade of the Rooms was until a few years ago largely hidden by hideous high iron railings.[26] When, after much consideration, the enclosure was adopted as the best site for a memorial statue of King Edward VII. the railings were removed and the space laid out as we see it to-day with the full length statue of the King in the centre. Two or three years ago Sir George A. Wills, Bt., bought the Rooms and presented them to the University as a Common Room; but they continue for the present to be available for certain public uses.

The man in khaki on a pedestal in the middle of the roadway is a memorial of the Gloucesters who fell in the South African War.[27] It was unveiled by the late Earl Roberts on March 4 1905. Some motorists are of opinion that it has become a danger to traffic and should be removed.

The Royal West of England Academy represents a considerable development of the Bristol Academy of Fine Arts founded early in 1845, but having no sufficient home until 1858.[28] The main supporter at the beginning was Mrs. Sharples,[29] who besides starting the Academy with a gift of

---


[24] The old Baptist College building was demolished in 1972.

[25] The Victoria Rooms at the time of its erection appears in "EARLIEST PHOTOGRAPHS", plates 85, 86.

[26] These railings are seen in the "1880's", plate 130.

[27] The Boer War Memorial (now on a roundabout) is seen in "TRAMS" plate 141.

[28] The R.W.A. in 1858 is illustrated in the "1850's", plate 73. The late President of the R.W.A., Lord Methuen, R.A., F.S.A., wrote the Preface to "1866–1860".

[29] Mrs. Sharples is featured in "ANN GREEN", Chapter 24.

£2,000, left the greater part of her estate at death in 1849 to the committee. With this bequest, £3,500, and the gifts of a very few the building was erected, but it was a very slow process educating the citizens to an adequate appreciation of the Academy. In 1882 Mr. Robert Lang, a generous friend, stated at the annual meeting that for the previous thirty years the public had not subscribed an annual average of £4. Several years ago a number of public-spirited men on the committee and off were successful in reviving interest in the Academy, Dame Janet Wills, the president, giving them generous support. The building was greatly improved, and the annual exhibitions are growing in importance.

In connection with the Academy, appropriately enough, is the Bristol School of Art[30] which follows with pride the career of a number of former pupils who have now become famous in the art world. The school is now a municipal institution.

The Diocesan Church House,[31] formerly the Queen's Hotel, we owe to the generosity of Mr. Samuel White, J.P. The House is fully and beautifully furnished and equipped for the administrative work of the diocese, with a valuable library. Here are to be found day by day clergy and laity engaged on a multitude of Church activities. There is probably no such scene of labour, so well accommodated, in any other diocese outside London.

---

[30] This organisation is now in new buildings at Bower Ashton as the Polytechnic College of Art.
[31] This is now in Great George Street.

Chapter 13

# QUEEN SQUARE

Plates 30, 44 and 45

Not everybody who knows Queen Square, not even those who spend a great portion of their lives in one of its houses—now most of them offices—knows how interesting is the history of this fine open space in the centre of the city. At one time it was the principal recreation ground of the citizens with its bull ring, bear-baiting, and its bowling green. Later it became the centre of a fashionable residential quarter. Now we think of it as a square of offices largely connected with shipping, with a statue of William III. in the centre, and as a convenient marshalling place for public processions to the Downs, when it is thought necessary to appeal to the imagination of the citizens on behalf of some great cause.[1]

The history of the spot carries us back to the beginnings of the abbey whose church survives as the cathedral of the diocese. The site is part of a large piece of marsh land which Robert Fitzhardinge, the twelfth-century founder of the abbey, included in its endowments. And when it was decided to make the Quay[2] in the thirteenth century, the abbot gave to Bristol the eastern portion of the marsh which became known as the town marsh, the western portion being the canons' marsh. The Corporation still own the eastern portion. We keep the old

---

[1] The environmentally disastrous bisection of the noblest square in the country was made in 1936-7 but plans for the future envisage traffic being re-routed elsewhere.

[2] The Quay to-day is called Quay Head, Colston Avenue, Broad Quay, and Narrow Quay.

name Canons' Marsh, and we have Marsh Street to remind us of the old name of the site of the square.

Laid out for building in 1699, and named in compliment to Queen Anne in 1702, the square was, in the days of the city walls, almost surrounded by the tidal rivers. In the 16th and 17th centuries, and long afterwards, it constituted, with Prince Street, the Bristol Marsh, and was a place where sheep grazed lazily in the day and the citizens passed a pleasant hour of a summer evening, though the Corporation did allow its green sward to be disfigured and its air to be tainted by house refuse.

Some benevolent citizen, whose enjoyment had been thus marred, stirred the Corporation unto action by making them trustees of a legacy bearing £4 interest per annum, and that £4 was to be spent on keeping the marsh clean. Two years afterwards (1611) a committee was charged with the duty of keeping the marsh decent and beautiful, and they took the graziers' rents and spent them on beautifying the place. In 1622 "merchants and gentlemen were allowed to recreate themselves at bowles," the committee finding and enclosing a site. This proved a profitable venture to the Corporation, and is a very early example of municipal trading. In 1631 a pair of stocks was added for the benefit of the unruly saunterers.

The marsh was evidently one of Bristol's beauty spots, for it is on record that visitors admired it, and wrote of it as a very delightful place, with pleasant and tree-sheltered walks and a bowling green open to the use of the wealthy and gentle—not the poor, be it observed, unless they were gentle. The bowling green was ruthlessly destroyed in 1643 when it became necessary to form batteries on the spot to defend the city against the Royalist forces. Some years later the wealthy and gentle got up a public subscription and with the money restored their green the Corporation in 1660 granting a lease of the site for £12 per annum. A tavern, disguised under the name of The Lodge, was close at hand for the bowlers. At a still later date the rent was increased by two capons, or 5s. paid to the Mayor in consideration of £60 spent on improvements of the bowling green, not I imagine out of the Mayor's private pocket.

Two years after the date of the lease just mentioned is this interesting entry in the City Audit Book: "The Chamberlain asks allowance for the trees blown down in the Marsh, belonging to him by custom time out out of mind as a perquisite of his

office; they being worth above £30, but sold under-hand at
£22." One may be sure that the Chamberlain received the £8
difference, if no more. Besides bowling, bull-baiting was
provided for those who thought bowling too tame; and a bull
ring was maintained in the square until houses came. Then the
ring was removed to St. Jude's and fixed on the spot where the
parish church now stands.

It was the impecuniosity of the Corporation which induced
them in March 1670 to direct a survey of the void ground in
the Marsh with a view to the erection of residences "by persons willing to accept leases of the same for five lives. Rent
reserved 12d. per foot at least for the frontage." There appears
to have been no great eagerness to take building plots, for it
was not until 1699 that a proposal to erect a dwelling-house
was presented, and then the Rev. John Reade, incumbent of
St. Nicholas, submitted a request to the Mayor for a site for a
vicarage. The Mayor, John Bachelor, draper, brought the
matter before the Council, and said if it was granted he believed
that other plots would be applied for; the Marsh, in fact, was
ripe for building. The Council agreed and appointed a committee to manage the estate. Probably St. Nicholas Vicarage
was not only the first house in Queen Square, as the Marsh
became, but the first wholly brick dwelling erected in Bristol.[3]
The Council insisted on this material, as among other qualities
it was less combustible than timber. Mr. Sheriff Hollidge, who
was Sheriff one year and Mayor the next, built the second house,
taking, indeed, three plots of land and paying £100 for the
bowling green lodge. He built several of the houses on the
south side of the square. Captain Woodes Rogers—the man
who discovered Alexander Selkirk, the original of Robinson
Crusoe, and who commanded the famous expedition sent out
by the Government in 1717 to crush the pirates of the Bahamas
—built two houses and lived in one which was afterwards No.
19. It was demolished with two others to make a site for the
Docks Offices. Other prominent citizens followed into the
Square. In 1781 the house built by Alderman Christopher
Shuter at the east end of the north side, in 1711, was bought for a
Mansion House for £1,350, £2,400 being spent on alterations.

The vicar of St. Nicholas completed his house in 1701, and

---

soon after Queen Anne came to the throne in the following year she paid her visit to Bristol (from Bath, where she was taking the waters for gout). There was tremendous rejoicing, and to keep fresh the memory of so great a day in local history "the square now building in the Marsh" was called Queen Square. One regrets that the Corporation did not look a little further ahead and name it Queen Anne Square.

When, in 1712, Queen Square had become fashionable as a place of residence, two ropewalks in the immediate neighbourhood were bought up and suppressed. In one case the property belonged to the Merchant Venturers, who would not sell unless 23 years were added to their 58 years' lease of the wharfage dues. The condition was accepted, a modification being that any member of the Corporation might have the Merchants' Hall for the purposes of "any publick feast or entertainment."

Michael Miller, merchant, lived and traded at No. 15, Queen Square—the house still stands—and in 1734 David Hume, historian and philosopher, then just 21, went into Miller's service as a clerk. Hume records that in a few months he found that "scene totally unsuited" to him. Miller was not well educated, but he was very successful in business. Hume irritated him by presuming to correct the grammar and style of his business letters. "I tell you what, Mr. Hume," exclaimed his master, "I have made £20,000 by my English and won't have it mended." Hume himself was by no means a writer of faultless English.

At No. 19, Woodes Rogers's former house, resided Joseph Smith, who was Burke's host during the famous election of 1774, when Cruger and Burke were returned. Burke acknowledged the kindness of his host and hostess by ordering of Richard Champion a china tea service bearing the Smith arms and Mrs. Smith's initials "S.S." In 1876 the teapot belonging to this set fetched £74 16s. at auction; a cup and saucer over ten years later realised £55. Another of Burke's hosts was Alderman John Noble, a Newfoundland merchant. In a letter to his wife on November 2nd 1774, Burke says: "I write from Mr. Noble's (of the Corporation), who is one of our very best friends, and this day gave us a very handsome dinner to which the committee and their ladies were invited. Two enemies, I think very willingly to be reconciled, were also invited. I begin to breathe, though my visits are not half over.

However, I dispatch them at a great rate. Two days more will, I think, carry me through most of them. The visits will then be over. The dinners would never end. But we close the poll of engagements next Saturday."

Sir Nathaniel Wraxall, author of "Historical Memoirs of My Own Time" and other works, was the son of a Bristol merchant and was born in Queen Square in 1751. His criticisms and anecdotes of notabilities brought forth many protests, and the Edinburgh Review published this premature epitaph on him:—

> Men, measures, scenes, and facts all
> > Misquoting, misstating,
> > Misplacing, misdating,
> Here "lies" Sir Nathaniel Wraxall.

There is not much doubt that Sir Nathaniel was more truthful than discreet. Burke, however, he never allowed to be as great as he really was. He praised his oratory and scholarship, but said Burke never knew when to sit down, "though warned by the clamorous vociferation of the House to restrain or to abbreviate his speeches ... His personal qualities of temper and disposition by no means corresponded with his intellectual endowments." In one of his travel books he offended the Russian Ambassador and suffered a fine of £500 and six months' imprisonment as a result. He died at Dover in 1831.

In Matthews's Directory for 1793–4 I find the following to be resident in Queen Square: Rev. George Hicks (Church of England); Godfrey Lowe, surgeon; Biggs and Popham, merchants; Richard Bright, No. 27, merchant; Mary Bundy, No. 20, lodging-house; William Butler, merchant; Lancelot Cowper, merchant; Edward Cropper, merchant; Gilford Davis, carpenter and builder; Ann Dyer, lodging-house; John Eames, No. 9, wine merchant; David Evans, gentleman; Philip Furse, No. 17, merchant; George Philip, No. 36, porter brewer; Richard Hayward, ship block maker; M. H. and R. Hunter, merchants; Mary Jenkins, No. 47, lodging-house; Philip Jones, merchant; John M'Cullom, No. 42, merchant; Philip John and William Miles, merchants; John Page, No. 59, merchant; Robert Salmon, No. 11, gentleman; John Waring, merchant; John James Wason, merchant; John Fisher Weare, merchant; and Ortando Wells, No. 17.

The equestrian statue of William III. which is a work by Rysbrach, was not erected without a good deal of feeling which extended far beyond the city. The Whig party in London raised a large sum for a statue there in the autumn of 1731, but the Common Council, the majority of whom were Tories, refused to grant a public site. This refusal, says Latimer, excited the Bristol Whigs to demonstrate their city's loyalty to the Revolution settlement, and they memorialised the Council asking for a site for the statue "to the memory of our great and glorious Deliverer, William III.," to be raised by public subscription. The Council not only replied that the statue could be placed in the centre of Queen Square, but they voted £500 toward the cost, offering to increase the amount if it were required. The Society of Merchant Venturers voted £300, and in September 1733 the foundations were laid in the Square, but it was not until three years later that the statue was on the site, and then it was found that a further £500 was needed, which the Council provided. Rysbrach's fee was £1,800, and the statue is judged to be one of his finest works; though the Jacobites, who were vocal if not numerous in the city, long continued to vent their spleen over the matter. Not many years after the statue was completed the City Chamberlain wrote (April 1749) to the sculptor to say that his work was in danger of total decay "unless some speedy and effectual means were used to repair it." Rysbrach denied liability and the Council, to the annoyance of the Jacobites, spent £111 on repairs to the statue and its pedestal. Perhaps this was the occasion on which the lead recently discovered amongst the bronze, was used. There has been some correspondence in our columns of late about the condition of the statue, and as a consequence it has been examined and the report is that while the corrosion is doing no particular harm, their are pieces of lead in the work which make repair desirable.[4]

I was interested and pleased to see in The Times Literary Supplement the other week a spirited protest by Mr. Hugh Walpole against what he regarded as a "contemptuous little notice" in that journal of a new story by Mr. Stanley Weyman, who was twenty years ago, as Mr. Walpole truly says, "the acknowledged head in England of a certain school of fiction"—

---

(4) The statue is now cleaned periodically; King William was evacuated to Badminton for safety in the 1939–1945 War.

the school of the historical romance.  I was pleased because of Mr. Walpole's generosity, and because one of the latest of Mr. Stanley Weyman's historical romances was "Chippinge," which has a strong Bristol flavour, not always suspected, I fear, from the title which the author chose.  "Chippinge" is a story of the Reform of 1831.  It describes Sir Robert Vermuyden's rotten borough (Malmesbury), which until 1832 returned two members to the House of Commons; had done so for so long that Sir Robert could not bring himself to believe that the town would willingly part with its privilege, for, though it was enjoyed vicariously, he paid £30 a year to the nine leading members of the Corporation, took a number of people off the rates, and set the beer taps going at election times.

One of the principal figures in the romance is Bristol's Recorder, Sir Charles Wetherell, and the Bristol Riots[5] are vividly described, in particular the scene in Queen Square.  It was there that the mischief first broke out—when on that Saturday morning, October 29th 1831, Sir Charles Wetherell, the Recorder, went in procession as usual to the Mansion House.  He reached there, through a hooting crowd, in safety, and all might have been well if the authorities—i.e., the special constables—had displayed anything approaching tact and reason.  But they had been hit by a few stones, and their blood was up.  They went for the crowd, and, as is so often the case, innocent spectators suffered most.  The crowd then had its turn.  Down came the Mansion House railings (which served as weapons), and smash went the windows, even one of the constables being frightened by threats into flinging his staff through one of the panes.  The Mansion House was soon at the mercy of the mob.  The costly furniture was shockingly maltreated, and the preparations for a civic feast went down the wrong throats.  The unpopular Recorder made an undignified flight over the roof into a stable, and finally to Newport. Troops appeared in the evening under Lieut.-Col. Brereton. The wrecking of the Mansion House was stopped, and its besieged occupants demanded that the Square should be cleared.  Col. Brereton tried gentle methods and was received by the crowd with cheers. But they would not go home.  The magistrates pressed him to clear the Square by force, and at

---

about 11 p.m. he directed Captain Gage, of the 14th Hussars, to do so. The rioters fled before the flat of the sabres, but returned immediately. Still, there was a quieting down for a time in the Square.

It was next found that the Council House was receiving attention at the hands of the rioters, and it was in dealing with them that the exasperated soldiers fired their first shots. Meantime, in the Square, the 250 special constables had dwindled to a dozen, and soon after daybreak on the Sunday morning the rioters came back to the Square. Finding the guarding forces absent or much reduced, the rioters resumed operations, recaptured the Mansion House, and threw the furniture out in the Square. The Mayor (Mr. C. Pinney) escaped with Major Mackworth along the roofs of several houses, and left via the Custom House for the Guild Hall. The crowd soon got to the wine cellar, and shortly afterwards men, women, and boys, mad drunk or helplessly intoxicated, were to be seen by the score. News of the free "drunk" spread, and brought all the inhabitants of slum-land to Queen Square. While this saturn-alia was in full swing, Col. Brereton came upon the scene; but he refused to use firearms, and said his troops wanted rest. The mob cheered the Dragoons, but hooted and ultimately stoned the Hussars, who had fired upon them at the Council House. Col. Brereton thereupon sent the Hussars to Keynsham, for which the crowd in the Square cheered him again. He talked suavely to the people, but though they stopped the plunder they continued the carousel. Judging by the general behaviour of the better class of citizens—who went to church as usual when the bells summoned them—they knew but little of the remarkable scene in the Square—a fact which Latimer attributes in part to the isolated position of the Square, and to the general unpopularity of everybody connected with the Mansion House.

The impotent civic and military authorities discussed what should be done, but disagreed for hours, and the mob in the Square decided to release those of their number who had been arrested, and also to let out of the Bridewell the prisoners sent there by the Recorder, who had the powers of a Judge of Assize. This was duly accomplished, and then the gaol was emptied, the five or six hundred rioters being thus considerably recruited. One party—"a mere handful," according to the

Bristol Mirror, rushed up to the Bishop's palace at the rear of the Cathedral. There is no doubt whatever that but for the pluck of the verger, William Phillips,[6] who, supported by a few citizens, chiefly Nonconformists, bravely faced the mob and shut the doors, much damage would have been done to the interior of the church. In the late Dean Pigou's time a memorial tablet was placed to put on record the verger's courage. He could not, however, save the palace or the library, where the rioters wrought much damage, destroying books and documents, and burning the palace so effectually that it was never restored[7] and remains to-day a monument of the savagery of the mob and the incompetency of the military.

An outbreak of fire in Queen Square drew the troops from College Green, and when they reached the Square they saw the palace well alight. The fire raged at each place, and by midnight all the houses in the Square, from the Mansion House to the Custom House, and including both, were sacked and burnt. "High above, dyeing the Floating Basin crimson, the Palace showed in a glow of fire; fire which seemed to be on the point of attacking the Cathedral, of which every pinnacle and buttress, with every chimney of the old houses clustered about it, stood out in the hot glare," says the novelist. And of the fire in the Square: "The whole of the north side . . . and half of the west side—full thirty lofty houses—were in flames, or sinking in red-hot ruin." . . . Tipsy groups, singing and dancing delirious jigs to the music of falling walls, pillagers hurrying in ruthless haste from house to house, or quarrelling over their spoils, householders striving to save a remnant of their goods from dwellings past saving," all made way for a charming girl who was bringing her invalid mother out of a burning house to the shelter of the side of the statue of William III., which was least subject to the ugly rushes caused by the fall of a roof or a rain of sparks.

The fire at the Custom House got such a rapid hold that some carousers in the rooms were compelled to jump out of the windows and were hurt or killed; others stayed and were roasted the accounts say. Charles Kingsley, who as a boy was at a

---

[6] This courageous worthy appears in "ANN GREEN", plates 37, 38 and page 182.

[7] The remaining ruins of the palace were demolished in 1963 to make way for a new hall for the Cathedral School. See "ANN GREEN", plates 35, 39.

school kept by the Rev. William Knight, rector of St. Michael's, when lecturing in Bristol in 1858, said he received in Bristol his first lesson in social science. It was when, one memorable Sunday afternoon in the sullen autumn rain and fog, he saw "through the fog a bright mass of flame—almost like a half-risen sun." That was a new gaol on fire, the prisoners having been set free . . . The flame increased, multiplied at one point after another, till by 10 o'clock that night one seemed to be looking down upon Dante's Inferno, and to hear the multitudinous moan and wail of the lost spirits surging to and fro amid the sea of fire." On the Tuesday or the Wednesday following he went to Queen Square and saw "a still more awful sight"—the ruins of noble buildings and a ghastly row of fragments of corpses.

The plunderers sold their ill-gotten gains in the Square to anybody who cared to buy at any price they would give. A piano was bought for 4s.—perhaps to be restored to its owner.

At the present Mansion House guests frequently ask to see a silver-gilt sixteenth century salver which belonged to the Mansion House in Queen Square. It is in 169 pieces skilfully rivetted together by a Bristol silversmith named Williams. He recovered the pieces from a man named Ives, who had stolen the salver and sought to destroy its identity by cutting it into fragments. Ives was transported for 14 years, and at the end of his sentence returned to Bristol, called at the Council House and coolly asked to be allowed to see the salver.[8]

It took the military until Monday morning to make up their minds to more drastic measures, the civil authority being useless. The Dragoons charged and a number of public-spirited citizens "went for" the looters in the burnt houses. The Hussars were brought in from Keynsham and other forces came from various places, Bedminster, Frome, Wincanton, and Gloucester. It was estimated that there were at least 250 casualties, many fatal, among the rioters and onlookers who had not the sense to keep away; the number was probably much larger, many of the cases being concealed for fear of the law when it should ultimately prevail. Over 4,000 special constables were now enrolled.

There followed trials of the rioters before the Lord Chief

---

1924: The author, Charles Wells, wearing the badge of office as President of Bristol Rotary Club, 1924–1925. [See page 5].

May 1924: The Bristol Pageant, held at Ashton Court and afterwards performed at the British Empire Exhibition, Wembley. This scene portrays Elizabeth I, who rode through the county town on a white horse in 1574, accompanied by her courtiers. [See page 150].

(31)    **1910: College Green:** children in sailor suits play on a summer's day round the 1851 Civic Cross; tall trees screen the shops.  [See page 115].

(32)    **1900–1907:  College Green:** the west side, mainly good Georgian houses, all demolished in the mid-1930's for the Council House.  Park street, off right, College Place off left.  [See page 102].

(33) **1900–1914: Queen's Road:** "Lennard's Corner", with Lennard's Shoes and Newbury & Spindler's furniture, blitzed 1940. Replaced by a modern store, whose future is uncertain. [See page 131].

(34) **1900–1914: Park Row,** the Prince's Theatre, built 1867, blitzed 1940, the saddest loss in local entertainment. Note the statues on the parapet.

**(35)    Pre-1910:   Queen's Road:** the School of Industry for the Blind in the Victorian Gothic style, now the site of the University.  [See page 132].

**(36)    c. 1920:   Bristol Grammar School,** an early aerial view: the Baptist College (top right); University Road (off right); Queen's Road shops (nearest camera); Queen's Avenue and Elmdale Road (left).  [See page 132].

**(37)** **October 1927: The Triangle Cinema,** which started as a skating rink, became a silent cinema, and converted to talkies in 1929. Dainty afternoon teas for the ladies, plus Ramon Novarro (who followed Rudolph Valentino—in popularity)—what more was needed? Blitzed in 1940, and now the site of Clifton Heights. [See page 133].

(38)   1912–1914: **Park Row:** The Coliseum, dance hall, skating rink, and where aeroplanes were made in the first war; blitzed 1940; note Provincial Motor Cab Co. Tel. 4040.

(39)   1905:  **Queen's Road,** towards the Victoria Rooms; Miss Pride's Servants' Registry on the left; corner property on the right, blitzed in 1940.  [See page 131].

(40) **1905: Great George Street:** The Bethesda Chapel, at the top, now part of the green space of Brandon Hill, following the blitz; this was George Muller's church, whose funeral service took place here, 14 March 1898.

(41) **pre 1905: The Victoria Rooms,** before the erection of Edward VII's statue and fountains in this neat little garden then behind high railings. [See page 133].

(42)   **1900–1910:  Whiteladies Gate:**   Imperial Hotel, extreme left; cabs and cabmen's shelter, tram No. 11, sand bin at the foot of the electric arc lamp (right), all unfamiliar to-day.  [See page 123].

(43)   **1900–1909:  Whiteladies Road:**   Oakfield Road (left), West Park (right), Tram No. 3 en route for Blackboy Hill; the Alexandra Drapers, a high class shop for Edwardian fashions.  The trees have gone.  [See page 123].

**(44)    30 March 1930:  Queen Square,** with Bell Lane leading to Welsh Back.  The 18th c. house and old  warehouses were demolished for the inner circuit road of the 1930's; St. Mary Redcliffe Church seen in the distance.

(45)    **23 July 1936: Queen Square**, just before the transformation caused by cutting the second largest square in Europe diagonally for the arterial road.  [See page 135].

(46)    **1933: The Merchants' Arms** at the corner of King Street and Prince Street, demolished to drive the inner circuit road through to Redcliffe Bridge.  The open touring car is a Bean of the 1920's.

(47)  c. 1930:  **Marsh Street:**  Merchants' Hall, the beautiful 18th c. headquarters of the Society of Merchant Venturers, lost in the blitz; the warehouse, left, is now rebuilt as a tower block, note the bull-nosed Morris radiator.  [See page 148].

(48)  c. 1900:  **King Street:** the Seamen's Almshouses, where old sea salts found peace ashore, looked after by the Merchant Venturers' Society.  Damaged in the blitz, the little houses have become old people's homes.  [See page 148].

(49)   1905–1914:  **Prince Street,** from the roof of the C.W.S. building (demolished 1974); horizon, left, the splendid dome of the General Hospital, a casualty of the blitz. Most buildings near the camera rebuilt since 1955.  [See page 154].

(50)   c. 1920:  **No. 40 Prince Street,** a fashionable mansion, built 1740–1, probably by Wm. Halfpenny (of the Coopers' Hall).  Seen here as the Health Offices; lost in the blitz.  [See page 154].

(51)    c. 1920:  **Prince Street,** the Assembly Rooms, probably by Wm. Halfpenny.  Scene of receptions and balls, redolent of Beau Brummel and Beau Nash, where the M.C. would not allow gentlemen to wear spurs.  Demolished in the 1920's; the C.W.S. extension built on the site in 1956.  [See page 154].

**(52)  1900–1914:  Hotwell Road,** looking into Dowry Square: Georgian houses and the 1872 Church of St. Andrew-the-Less, left, replaced by flats in the 1960's; distant houses now saved and restored; note butcher's boy, coalman's horse and cart, baker's cart, and tram 211.  [See page 157].

**(53)  4 March 1959:  Surrey Street, Brunswick Square:**  Surrey Villa, a Victorian fancy, demolished despite protests.  [See page 161].

**(54)** **June 1901: Broad Weir:** Taylor's 17th c. timber-framed building was a casualty in the 1942 daylight raid when three buses were hit. The old Crown public house gave way to new shops in 1957. Philadelphia Street, right, known affectionately as "Phily-I-Fi" Street. The site of the present-day Penn Street signals just off right. [See page 172].

(55)   **1888–1892: The Drawbridge of 1868–1892**; "Q" shed 1879–1892; Baldwin Street, cut in 1881; the BTCC horse tram has seven windows; the time is 12.55 p.m.  [See page 172].

(56)   **1896 or 1897: St. Augustine's Bridge,** replacing the drawbridge; horse trams round the Tramways Centre; a bandstand on the Cenotaph site; note crossing sweeper's path of duty astride Anchor Road.  [See page 172].

Justice and other members of a special Commission appointed by the Government—instead of the Recorder, who had been suggested by the Corporation as a fit judge!  The trials took place in January 1832, and of 102 prisoners tried 81 were convicted, five being executed and 26 on whom the death sentence was passed were transported for long terms; the rest of the convicted received sentences of imprisonment.

Colonel Brereton committed suicide in his home in St. George during his Court Martial.  The Mayor was tried by the Queen's Bench in October 1832 for neglect of duty, and was honourably acquitted, a verdict which led to the withdrawal of the Government's indictment against his fellow-justices, the aldermen.

The damage done by these riots led to the passing of an Act of Parliament to provide for compensation for losses through rioting and the improvement of municipal police forces.  Under the Compensation Act a dozen Commissioners were appointed to deal with 121 actions against the city authorities to recover damages to a total of £150,000—mostly for furniture destroyed. The claims from owners and residents in respect of losses in Queen Square were settled at much reduced figures, as this list will show:—

| Claimant and Property | Claimed. | Paid. |
|---|---|---|
| F. T. Barnard, 3, Queen Square | £2,000 | £722 |
| J. Barrett, 57, Queen Square | 1,490 | 855 |
| B. Bickley, 54, Queen Square | 3,500 | 2,042 |
| Cowbridge and Williams, Avenue | 1,000 | 400 |
| Cooke and Turner, 51, Queen Square (rear of) | 1,000 | 327 |
| T. Crocker, 52, Queen Square | 1,100 | 52 |
| R. T. Coombe, 6 and 7, Queen Square | 2,900 | 2,050 |
| Daniel and Haythorne, 51, Queen Square | 1,500 | 950 |
| W. Gibbons, 54, Queen Square, &c. | 4,000 | 1,750 |
| Martha Harford, Excise Avenue | 1,600 | 908 |
| Maria Jones, 50, Queen Square, | 1,600 | 930 |
| R. Lambert, 45, Queen Square | 1,150 | 1,005 |
| Langley and Harding, 43, 44, and 62 Queen Square, &c. (shares in) | 1,700 | 660 |
| P. J. Miles, 61, Queen Square | 3,500 | 1,312 |
| Mogg and Bartlett, Avenue | 1,000 | 493 |
| J. Morgan, 3 Queen Square | 1,690 | 1,000 |
| C. Pinney (Mayor), Mansion House | 2,000 | 714 |
| J. Room, 61, Queen Square | 3,000 | 1,172 |
| H. Rumley, 46, Queen Square (share) | 1,779 | 605 |
| J. Richardson, 45, Queen Square | 2,000 | 381 |
| H. B. Smith, 59 and 60, Queen Square | 4,649 | 2,938 |
| W. C. Stephens, 53, Queen Square | 1,600 | 309 |

| | | |
|---|---|---|
| T. Sheppard, 5, Queen Square .............. | 1,100 .. | 712 |
| W. Strong, 63, Queen Square ................ | 2,000 .. | 336 |
| R. Thomas, 43, 44, and 52, Queen Square, &c. (shares in) ................................ | 1,700 .. | 285 |
| M. M. J. and E. Vigor, 6, Queen Square ...... | 1,000 .. | 450 |
| T. Webb and Co., 4, Queen Square .......... | 2,000 .. | 652 |
| G. Warrall, 5, Queen Square ................ | 2,000 | 1,016 |
| J. Tilladam, 4, Queen Square ................ | 1,000 (abated by death) | |
| S. Webb, 47 and 48, Queen Square .......... | 1,800 (abated by death) | |

In 1833 it was resolved to rebuild the Mansion House if an adjoining property could be obtained to allow of a larger house, but that was found impossible and a private residence in Great George Street was converted into a Mansion House at considerable cost, to be closed when the Corporation was reformed under the Act of 1835. Bristol was Mansion House-less from 1836 until May, 1874, when Alderman Thomas Proctor executed a deed of gift under which he transferred to the city his house on Clifton Down, which is still used as the Lord Mayor's official residence. For many years the judges of assize went to the Clifton Down Hotel as the guests of the city rather than go to the Mansion House, but the hotel having been "commandeered" by the Ministry of Pensions a few years ago, the judges have since slept at the Mansion House.

Another of the effects of the riots was to deprive Bristol of its ancient Assizes, which had been held twice a year before the Recorder, and it took more than 50 years of effort to get them back. Sir Charles Wetherell held no assize between 1831 and 1835 and the Municipal Corporations Act of the latter year took away Bristol's privilege. Then it became a question of new Law Courts, and in 1865 Queen Square was favoured as a site. Ultimately the site of the old Guild Hall was adopted and the new Courts were opened in 1870. I wonder if it will ever be thought well to restore the game of bowls to Queen Square. That would certainly be more agreeable to history than the recent proposal to park motor vehicles there.[9]

---

[9] What would Charles Wells have thought of double yellow lines, wavy lines, beacons, meters, parking signs and traffic wardens?

Chapter 14

# KING STREET & PRINCE STREET

Plates 46, 47, 48, 49, 50 and 51

King Street and Prince Street, like Queen Square, have long since ceased to be fashionable residential quarters, but some of the houses and other buildings remain to remind us of that long ago, and it is well worth while when in the neighbourhood of Queen Square to look at these two thoroughfares now so generally given up to commerce and professional work. Of the smaller kind a good example of the dwellings in King Street is the row which includes Llandoger Tavern.[1]

The first building to be erected in what is now King Street was St. Nicholas Almshouses which stand on a piece of land which formed part of the Marsh described a fortnight ago, and were erected about 1652. It was in June that year that the parishioners obtained the plot from the Council under the city wall, in the Marsh, near Back Gate, for a chief rent of 6s. 8d. a year. Four years later they took an additional bit of land, which included one of the round towers on the wall.[2] The development of the street was not rapid for until 1663, Latimer says, "the almsfolk had a pleasant outlook on the green Marsh and the busy Avon."

In March of that year the Council decided to lay out the street "from Weare's house to the Marsh Gate," and later the thoroughfare became known by its present name. The land

---

[1] The then Llandoger *Tavern* subsequently became the Llandoger *Trow* (the old name is visible in the "1890's", plate 89).

[2] Part of this bastion came to light in the restoration of the almshouses, and is illustrated in "TRADITION", plate 22.

was let on leases for five lives, or for 41 years certain at a reserved rent of 1s. to 1s. 6d. per foot frontage, the lessees agree-
ing to erect buildings of uniform architecture, but in fact they
erected according to their own particular taste. Nevertheless
some handsome houses were put up.

At the further end of the street, and on the same side as the
St. Nicholas Almshouses is the quadrangle forming the Merchants' (or St. Clement's) Almhouse.[3] Its history goes back to
the early half of the 15th century when a Guild of the Bristol
Mariners was founded for the purpose of erecting a chapel in
honour of the blessed St. Clement and St. George, on a site in
the Marsh adjoining a tower on the town wall (subsequently
the site of the King Street Library), maintaining a priest and
twelve poor seamen. The present almshouse and Merchants'
Hall now stand on the land. The chapel was erected by the
Corporation to increase the opportunities for divine worship,
and (quite irregularly) passed in 1550 under the Act dissolving
charities, to Sir Ralph Sadlier and another. A little later,
however, the Corporation was in possession, and a reference in
1561 to the chapel and St. Clement's Almshouse suggests that
the property had passed to the Society of Merchants some time
earlier. The almshouse was enlarged in 1699 by the help of
Edward Colston, who gave the land—another portion of the
site of the old town wall.

The chapel apparently served as the Hall for a considerable
period in the seventeenth century, and the present Hall seems
to have been erected in a piecemeal fashion.[4] At the beginning
of the eighteenth century alterations were made to the chapel
to increase its accommodation. Two new rooms—the Great
Room and the Withdrawing Room—were added about 1719,
and soon after "a handsome way . . . at the entrance of our
Hall" was decided upon. This involved the demolition of
some old houses. Two years later the frontage to King Street
was re-built, and the iron gates were erected at the entrance in
Marsh Street. In 1788 the reconstruction of the Hall was
resolved upon, the work occupying some years and costing
£6,000, of which £542 was for chandeliers and lamps. The

---

<sup></sup>(3) This is illustrated in "TO-DAY", 4th Ed., plate 184.

(4) The Hall, blitzed in 1940, is seen in the "1890's", plate 69, and "1914–1900",
plate 134.

present committee-room and the treasurer's office are mid-nineteenth century additions.

The Hall contains some portraits[5] of sovereigns and past masters, and has been the scene of many notable gatherings—not merely banquets and balls, but meetings to promote various causes of national or local importance, the Merchants being ever ready to help in welcoming distinguished guests to Bristol or furthering good movements. The annual meetings of the Chamber of Commerce are held in the Hall, a survival of the times when the Master was ex-officio President of the Chamber.

This is not a history of the Merchant Venturers and therefore I say nothing of the work and influence of "the Hall" in bygone days, and content myself with stating that it has adapted itself to the needs of the present times, sympathetically administering charities, and in particular promoting higher education.

One of the Bristolians who ought never to be forgotten is Robert Redwood, who informed the Council in December 1613 that he desired to give his "lodge near the Marsh" to the city as a home for a collection of books to be at the service of his fellow-citizens—a gift which was gratefully accepted. It seems likely that Redwood had been in communication with another Bristolian—the Archbishop of York (Dr. Tobias Matthew)—about the project, as his Grace speedily sent to Bristol a number of valuable books out of his own library "for the free use of the merchants and shopkeepers." The Council resolved, in January 1616, to pay "him that keepeth the new erected library" 40s. per annum. I gather that that refers to the new use of the house and not to the building itself. Being hard up in 1691 the Council decided to cease payment of the salary when the existing librarian died, and to let part of the premises as a dwelling-house, storing the books in the other part. Up to this time the librarian had dwelt on the premises. This, the earliest public library but one (Norwich) in the country, proved highly successful and soon more accommodation was required. In April 1634 it was reported at a meeting of the Council that for the extension of the premises "Mr. Richard Vickris hath freely given a parcel of ground adjoining the said library."

---

[5] Rescue work in the war is illustrated in "BLITZED", plate 69.

The Council voted £30 for the additional building and repair
of the old, the work to be superintended by Mr. George Butcher
(or Boucher, or Bowcher), who a few years later was to make
history by suffering "martyrdom" for his Royalist principles,
as we are being reminded in the Bristol Pageant.[6]  An interesting entry in the Corporation accounts is a payment of £3 17s.
6d. for $5\frac{1}{2}$ dozen book chains for the Library.  Latimer suggests
that "the portliness of most of the volumes" made chains super-
fluous as a protection from theft, but the authorities of that day
took no risks.  The Archbishop's books are now at the Central
Library in College Green.  The early librarians were parsons,
usually incumbents of St. Leonards[7] or, when that church was
demolished, of St. Nicholas, and in December 1725 the librarian,
the Rev. Robert Clarke, who described himself as "librarian by
will of the donor," made strong representations to the Council
about the ruinous condition of the building.  A committee was
appointed to report, but nothing happened until 1738, when,
at the instance of the Recorder, another committee took
action, removed the books to the Council House and recommended that the library premises be rebuilt.  This was done on
an extended scale, the work being completed in 1740, Alderman
Michael Becher being credited with the gift of the fine mantelpiece,[8] believed to have been carved by Grinling Gibbons.
There was a wing added in 1789 at the cost of the Library
Society formed in 1772 with Bishop Newton as president.[9]
The society had managed to obtain possession of the premises,
and soon it became an impertinence for a non-subscriber to
that society to venture to use even the books that were originally
meant for the free use of the citizens.  There was naturally
much feeling aroused over this wrangling by this new society
for the promotion of literature.

The story of the Library Society is well told in a little book
by Mr. Charles Tovey, who was a member of the Town Council
from 1847 to 1862 and who, with other members, secured an
investigation of the whole position.  It was found that the
Library Society had come to regard the library as their property

---

[6] This was an event of some consequence in 1924, and therefore fresh in the
mind of Charles Wells.

[7] St. Leonards, demolished in 1766, stood at the corner of Corn Street and
St. Stephen Street.

[8] This mantelpiece is illustrated in "1914–1900", plate 82.

[9] This building is seen in the "1880's", plate 64, and "1914–1900", plate 136.

and had acted accordingly. They had persuaded the Council, which comprised some of their fellow-members, to spend public money on the repair and maintenance of the library during their occupation and to pay part of the librarian's salary, and this at a time when non-members of the society were completely excluded from use of the library established for their benefit.

At last the society over-reached themselves. They requested the Corporation, in 1826, "to remove the city books from the city shelves in order to make room for books belonging to the society." By this time the Council had woke up to the situation, and declined to comply with the request. But it was not until 1854 that the Corporation regained possession of the building. Then they paid £630 to the Library Society on account of the new wing, and the society removed their 2,000 volumes to rooms in Bishop's College, Queen's Road.[10] The Corporation made the necessary alterations and re-opened the library in September 1856 with Mr. George Pryce as Librarian. While filling that post Mr. Pryce brought out his "Popular History of Bristol."[11] There were soon, by gifts and other means, large additions to the books, and from that old library, founded three centuries ago, have grown the fine branch libraries and the great Central Library next to the Cathedral, this last provided by a bequest of £50,000 from the estate of Mr. Vincent Stuckey Lean, who died in 1899. This handsome building—perhaps rather more handsome than convenient from the administration point of view—was opened in June 1906.[12] The executors of Mr. Lean added to his munificence by presenting his library of 5,000 books and pamphlets on his hobby of folklore, British and foreign. The Bristol Room contains a priceless collection of Bristoliana and the reputed Grinling Gibbons mantelpiece, as well as the old presses from King Street. In the Reference Library are some rare fifteenth and sixteenth century books and some good examples of illuminated manuscripts. The Old Library is now used by the Corporation for the administration of its Taxation Department.

---

(10) This building is seen in the "1880's", plate 118.

(11) Extracts from the interesting writings of George Pryce appear in:— "1866–1860", pages 57, 58, 59; "BRISTOL'S EARLIEST PHOTOGRAPHS", page 16; "ANN GREEN", page xiv.

(12) This fine library, designed by Charles Holden, is illustrated in "TO-DAY", 4th Ed., plate 49. It was extended in 1967, and further extensions are possible.

The Library Society found a home at the Museum in Queen's Road, and remained there until 1905, when the Corporation took possession of that institution. For a time the society's books were lodged with Messrs. Georges, booksellers, at the top of Park Street, but not for long. The society was soon wound up and the books were sold.

The Theatre Royal was erected in King Street between December 1764, when the foundation-stone was laid, and May 30, 1776 when the first performance was given. There was so much Puritanical hostility to secular play-acting at that time that the managers dare not announce a play for the opening. They said they were going to give "a concert of music" for the benefit of the Royal Infirmary, and that at an interval "a Specimen of Rhetoric diversified in the several characters of a Comedy called 'The Conscious Lovers.'" But this was an extra and gratis, the prices of 4s. for boxes, 2s. 6d. pit, and 1s. 6d. gallery, were for the concert. An epilogue, written by David Garrick, was spoken by Mr. William Powell, one of the three managers and an actor who gained great popularity when at last plays were permitted. At his early death the whole city sorrowed, and he was buried in the Cathedral, where a memorial was erected by his widow to him as "the best of husbands, fathers, and friends."

There are notable names associated with this old theatre. Mrs. Siddons played there, but without proving a great draw. In the nineteenth century, under William Macready and J. H. Chute, many others who became stars appeared on the boards— Mrs. Kendal, the Misses Marie Wilton, Kate and Ellen Terry, Henrietta Hodson, and Madge Robertson are among the women who achieved national fame. Then there were, among men, Macready himself, Charles Matthews, Henry Irving, and George and William Rignold.

Silver tickets giving a right to free admission to every performance were issued to 48 persons who had subscribed £50 capital. Some spurious tickets got into circulation, but they were difficult to identify. A story is told of the holder of a ticket being refused admission on the ground that the ticket was a forgery. Thereupon a solicitor voluntarily offered to test the matter, and was successful. For his services—three attendances at the play—he sent in a surprising bill of £15. In 1777 a Royal patent for the theatre was obtained, and under it the theatre was maintained until quite recent years.  At the present time the house is closed,[13] and the proprietors—a number of shareholders—are seeking to sell it, hoping that it may continue a place of entertainment.

Latimer notes that the migration of many of the leading families to Queen Square led to the abandonment of the old Assembly Rooms in the Pithay.  About 1737 Messrs. John Wallis, John Summers, and Roger Elletson succeeded in establishing winter assemblies at the Merchants' Hall.  An incidental notice in a London paper of December 1738 states that the Bristol assemblies were held in Coopers' Hall, then near Corn Street, and balls were probably given in one or other of these buildings until the conversion into an assembly room of the theatre in St. Augustine's.

John Wood, senior, architect of the Exchange, describes the hall of the Coopers' Company as a "shattered old building".  It was bought by the Corporation and demolished about 1742, in order to widen the passage on the western side of the Exchange.  The Coopers' Company refused to part with their property for the £1,500 cash offered by the Corporation, and insisted and obtained four houses in King Street and £900 cash.  On the site of the four houses the Coopers erected their new hall from the designs of William Halfpenny, who published a view of the building in 1744.

Changing times bringing with them a greater population and extension of trade made it impossible to force young men into the incorporated trade guilds with their strict ordinances, and as members died there were none to take their places. This change was very pronounced in the early decades of the eighteenth century, and by the end many of the guilds had died of inanition.  The Coopers, who obtained their first set of ordinances in 1493, went the way of the rest, and in February 1785 their hall was advertised for sale by auction.[14]  At the coronation of George IV, in July 1821, only the Pin Makers and Wire Workers' Companies survived to take part in a civic procession to service at the Cathedral.  Three years later Isaac

---

(13) For another crisis in the history of the Theatre, see "BLITZED", plate 169.
(14) The Coopers' Hall has become the splendid foyer of the Theatre Royal. See "TO-DAY", 4th Ed., plate 47.

Amos died, the last of the Merchant Taylors' Company, the man who re-elected himself as master year by year and took ten guineas for serving an extra time, twelve for his attendances at meetings, and two for auditing the accounts which he himself kept. After his death a trust was created to manage the estate, and the money used for the maintenance of the almshouse in Merchant Street. That house has just been closed, but the pensioners remain to be helped.

Prince's Street—which we now miscall Prince Street—was named after Prince George of Denmark, and the upper portion was made in the closing years of Queen Anne's reign. Mansions in the lower part did not begin to appear until 1725, and in that year John Becher, Henry Coombe and other wealthy merchants took leases of sites from the Corporation, and built houses on them. There are a few of these fine dwellings left.[15] The Public Health Department occupies one of the stateliest.[16]

Humphrey Hooke (Mayor 1629–30) built a house early in the seventeenth century near, if not on, the site subsequently chosen for the Assembly Rooms, and it was long regarded as one of the pleasantest residences in Bristol, being, for that reason, commonly used as a guest house for judges. Chief Justice North lodged there when Robert Aldworth (Mayor 1609–1610) was the tenant. Later John Romsey, Town Clerk, lived in the house and there received Judge Jefferys when he came to Bristol to hold the Bloody Assizes. Certain of our historians, John Evans the chief, have placed this house in King Street,[17] being misled by the fact that a smaller house in that street, which was demolished in our own time, bore the initials "J. R." The true site, Latimer points out, is minutely described in the Bargain Books of the Corporation. Aldworth was a familiar name in city affairs during the seventeenth century, and Aldworth's Quay was near to this house at the end of a lane which until recent years was known as Aldersky Lane,[18] really Aldsworth's Quay Lane.

John Wesley found Prince's Street a convenient place for preaching in the open-air and often took advantage of it.

The Assembly Rooms, Prince's Street, of which little remains

---

[15] Known as the Merchants' houses, they are illustrated in "TRADITION", plate 145. Sadly, their future is uncertain.
[16] This was No. 40 Prince Street, seen in plate 50.
[17] The so-called Romsey House is illustrated in "1879–1874", plate 99.
[18] This is illustrated in "1890's", plate 60.

to remind us of its imposing character, were erected in the middle of the eighteenth century on land partly occupied by four old houses belonging to the Coporation. The terms of the lease granted in March 1754 to Messrs. Cranfield Becher, John Heylyn, Morgan Smith, and others were that £400 be paid down, the rent to be £5 a year, and a fine of £100 on renewal of lease every fourteen years; the old buildings to be demolished and a large room erected in their place suited for public assemblies. The free use of the building seven times a year was reserved to the Corporation for the entertainment of Royal visitors. Hitherto this had been a privilege conceded at the Merchant Venturers' Hall, nearly opposite the site of the proposed new building.

One hundred and twenty £30 shares were issued on the tontine principle, and "the new Music Room," as it was called, was opened on Wednesday January 14, 1756, with a performance of "The Messiah," the orchestra being made up of performers from London, Oxford, Salisbury, Gloucester, Wells, Bath, and other places. Mr. Broderip was announced to give "a concerto on the organ." Tickets were 5s. each. The elegance of the room and the chandeliers were commented upon by a correspondent of Felix Farley's Bristol Journal. In March 1757 a two-day musical festival was held in the room, when "Judas Maccabaeus" and "The Messiah" were performed. Sheircliff's Guide of 1789 gives particulars of balls at the Assembly Rooms on alternate Thursdays, "Menuets" at 6.30, country dances at 8. No ladies to be admitted in hats. No children to dance menuets in frocks. The subscription for the season was two guineas, or for visitors 5s. each evening. James Russell, Esq., M.C., was ordered to close the dancing at 11 o'clock precisely.

The reluctance to support Bishop Butler's appeal for funds to build and endow a new church for the benefit of the spiritually destitute colliers of Kingswood, while money could be found for amusement, was the subject of satirical comment in the local press. Human nature remains much the same to-day as it was then.

There are many citizens who are old enough to remember lectures and various forms of entertainment being given in these Rooms, though they were even then declining in favour, as Queen Square and Prince's Street were already superseded

by Clifton as the fashionable residential quarters.  Eventually
the building was let as a warehouse,[19] and twelve years ago it
was dismantled and reduced to its present lowly state, with
little to suggest the glories of the eighteenth century, the
brilliant functions within and the walk home by torchlight
after the Master of Ceremonies stopped the dancing or sent
the diners away.

---

[19] Twelve years ago indicates 1912, therefore it must still have been standing
in June 1924; however, shortly afterwards it was demolished to about three feet
above the ground. The site remained empty for several decades. See plate 51.

# SOME HISTORIC SQUARES

**Plates 52 and 53**

In previous articles I have dealt with Queen Square at length and with one or two others less so. There are but few of the once-fashionable residential squares which have not succumbed in a greater or less degree to the call of the newer suburbs— around the Downs in particular. The consequence is that many of the fine old family mansions which were occupied by the grandfathers of citizens of to-day are now diverted to commerce —some as boot and shoe, or clothing or corset factories; some as offices.[1] They wear a faded look, but it is still possible to judge even from the exteriors what handsome, well-proportioned houses they were. Too many stairs, too little regard for labour-saving, no doubt, but still dignified and stately for all the rough usage to which they are now subjected and the absence of paint.

## DOWRY SQUARE

The earliest publicly-printed reference to Dowry Square[2] which Latimer found is dated February 4th 1727, when a "large new built house, with coach-houses, stables, etc., situate in the New Square in Dowry" was advertised to be let. The Square, says Latimer was not completed until many years afterwards. Many of the houses are still occupied as dwellings, the larger—some of them very fine—being let in tenements.

---

[1] Excepting the warehouses in Portland and Brunswick Squares, offices now dominate Dowry, Berkeley, and Queen Squares; very few private houses survive. Somerset and St. James's Squares were blitzed and demolished.
[2] This is illustrated in "TO-DAY" 4th Ed., plate 132.

The name suggests a provision for some widow belonging to an aristocratic family.

To me the most interesting house is No. 6, the one in the far corner looking diagonally across the enclosure to the right as you enter the Square from the Hotwell Road. The house is built so as to extend to two sides of the Square, and I am satisfied that it is the property which Dr. Thomas Beddoes took for his Pneumatic Institute to treat disease by inhalation. I quote Latimer's reference: "During the year 1793, Dr. Thomas Beddoes, who had distinguished himself as a Reader in Chemistry at the University of Oxford from 1788 to 1792, but had found further residence there impracticable owing to his sympathy with the French Republicans, settled in Clifton, with a view to establishing a Pneumatic Institute for the treatment of diseases by inhalation. The reputation of the new comer as a vigorous and original thinker was already considerable in cultivated circles, and his fame among the visitors to Clifton—among whom the Marquess of Lansdowne, Earl Stanhope, and Mr. Lambton, father of the first Earl of Durham were then conspicuous—soon spread among the Whig inhabitants. The apparatus for the intended experiment was constructed by James Watt, £1,500 of the outlay being contributed by Mr. Lambton and £1,000 by Thomas Wedgwood, who removed to Clifton to enjoy Beddoe's society. Southey and Coleridge were also close friends of the doctor, whose talents and philanthropy they warmly eulogised. The institution was at length opened in Dowry Square in 1798, and though it failed in its professed object it is memorable for having fostered the genius of young Humphrey Davy, who was engaged as assistant, and who there discovered the properties of nitrous-oxide gas in 1799, to Southey's enthusiastic delight. Dr. Beddoes closed the institution in 1801, and died in December 1808, at a moment, says Davy, when his mind was purified for noble affections and great works. 'He had talents which would have raised him to the highest pinnacle of philosophical eminence if they had been applied with discretion.'" It was Dr. Beddoes who organised a course of anatomical lectures at the Red Lodge by Mr. Francis C. Bowles and Mr. Richard Smith, two leading Bristol surgeons, a movement which resulted in the establishment of a School of Anatomy and so may be said to have laid the foundations of the Bristol Medical School of to-day.

When certain Bristolians were in a mood to mark certain houses which had a history, the intention was to put a tablet on the house in Dowry Square which had been the Pneumatic Institute. But doubts arose as to its identity, and so the tablet was placed on Dr. Beddoes's house, No. 3, Rodney Place, Davy being of the household. In that way two birds were killed with one stone; but I think that the house in Dowry Square should also be marked.[3] Cottle, who must have known, said the institution was in "the house in the corner, forming the north-east angle of the Square," and I remember pointing that out to the committee at the time they were looking for the house.

It was when he was living at Westbury-on-Trym (1798-9) that Southey made the acquaintance of Davy. In July of the following year, after leaving Westbury, Southey wrote a letter to his brother in which is this passage: "Oh, Tom! such a gas has Davy discovered, the gaseous oxyde! Oh, Tom! I have had some; it made me laugh and tingle in every toe and finger tip. Davy has actually invented a new pleasure for which language has no name. Oh, Tom! I am going for more this evening; it makes one strong and so happy! so gloriously happy! and without any after-debility, but instead of it in-creased strength of mind and body. Oh, excellent air-bag! Tom, I am sure the air of heaven must be in this wonder-working gas of delight."

When the waters of Clifton were at the height of their fame—that is, in the mid-eighteenth century—it was the fashion to hold public breakfasts and dances twice a week in the Long Room; and occasionally some private functions of the kind were arranged by hospitable visitors of distinction. For example, in June 1743 the Earl of Jersey entertained 150 of the aristocracy to breakfast, and two days later the Hon. Mr. Ponsonby gave a similar entertainment. So great was the demand on accommodation about this time that several large lodging-houses were built in Dowry Square, and a New Vauxhall Gardens laid out for the amusement of bathers and drinkers. A firm of London dealers in lace opened a branch shop to catch the custom of the wealthy throng of invalids in the Square. The price of general lodgings was 10s. a week in the summer and 5s. in the winter, boarding 16s.; servants half

---

[3] This has been done by the erection of a Civic Society plaque.

prices. The decline of the Hotwell began in the last decade of the century, and continued in spite of strenuous efforts to stay the decline, which was attributed to the rapacity of the management of the Pump Room and of the landladies. The old Pump Room, erected about 1696, was removed in 1822 to allow Bridge Valley Road to be made, giving better access to the Downs, and a new Pump Room was erected.[4] This venture came too late for any success, and in 1867, to permit of the widening of the river, the building was pulled down. This river improvement rendered the spring inaccessible for many years, and when the water was brought into reach again it was carried so far that the term "hot" became a misnomer. Due to the initiation of the late Sir George Newnes, the Clifton Grand Spa Hydro was opened in Prince's Buildings on March 31 1898, but it is now better known as a residential hotel than as a Pump Room.

Reference to local guides as recent as a century ago will show that the York Hotel in the Square was described for the benefit of visitors as "a very respectable and quiet family house." and that the principal resorts at the Hotwells included Dowry Square, Dowry Place, Dowry Parade, Chapel Row, Hope Square, Albemarle Row, and Granby Hill. For warm and sheltered residences Dowry Parade was one of the two or three places recommended.

The church of St. Andrew-the-Less was consecrated on September 24 1873.[5] It was erected on the site of Dowry Chapel, built in 1746 for the fashionable folk visiting the Hotwells to take the waters.[6] The Rev. William Cole, the Cambridge antiquary, was at the Hotwells in May 1746 when the chapel was in course of erection, and he made notes about it which are preserved, with other MSS. of his, at the British Museum. From these notes it appears that £50 was paid to Mr. Tully for the ground, and that the total outlay up to date was £259 6s. 4d.

Also for the convenience of visitors two of the Countess of Huntingdon's followers, Lady Henrietta Hope and Lady Glenorchy, built Hope Chapel on a slope above the Square now known as Hope Chapel Hill. This chapel, opened on

---

(4) Hotwell House is well seen in the "1850's", plate 107.
(5) St. Andrew-The-Less was demolished in 1963.
(6) For Dowry Chapel, see "1866–1860", plate 65.

August 31 1788, superseded the chapel which the Countess had fitted up in the old Assembly Room (formerly a theatre) that stood on the site of the Gas Company's offices in Colston Street.[7] Mr. Luke, whose wife wrote, "When I think of that Sweet Story" and other popular hymns for children, was at one time minister at Hope Chapel.

Clifton Dispensary, which is accommodated in one of the houses, was founded in 1812, and treats thousands of sick poor every year—residents of Clifton. There is a resident staff as well as an outside staff. The control of the dispensary rests with a committee of ladies and gentlemen who are deeply interested in their work.

Dr. John Nott lived in Dowry Square (No. 1, Chapel Row, really part of the square). He was of literary habits, and edited some of the poets, including Withers, thereby incurring the wrath of Charles Lamb, who castigated him with "Thou damned fool!" "O, eloquent in abuse! Niggardly where thou should'st praise, most negative Nott," and such-like phrases of comment.

## BRUNSWICK SQUARE

Five of the houses on the east side of Brunswick Square were built by a Tontine established in 1786. The cost was 5,000 guineas, divided into 100 shares of 50 guineas each, held by as many lives. Among the shareholders were some of the leading Quakers of the city—Edward Ash, John Cave, George Eaton, John P. Fry, John Godwin, John J. Harford, Edward Harwood, Abraham Ludlow, Thomas Mills, Joseph Were, and Matthew Wright. By 1860 the number of surviving lives was only five, and it was decided to ballot for the properties. The result was that Mrs. S. P. Anderson, of Henlade, took No. 7 (the largest house), Mr. R. Ash No. 8, Miss F. Wright No. 9, and Alderman R. H. Webb, who represented two lives, had Nos. 10 and 11. When laid out the Square was planted with elms, and a colony of rooks soon took up residence in them. In 1858 the trees had become dangerous and were cut down, the birds removing to the neighbourhood of Redland Court. About 40 years ago these trees also were cut down, so that houses could be built on the site.

---

[7] The original Countess of Huntingdon Chapel is illustrated in the "1890's", plate 30.

In Brunswick Square is the old burial ground of the Unitarians. The headstones there bear the names of men who were prominent citizens in by-gone days, the days when many of the aldermen and magistrates and councillors attended service at Lewin's Mead Meeting. Only once have I witnessed an interment there, and that was in January, 1904, when all that remained of John Latimer was laid there.[8] In an eloquent address at the graveside the Rev. Ambrose N. Blatchford spoke of Latimer's skill in drawing back "the ever thickening curtain of the past." William James Müller, the artist, whose works have made him famous throughout the land, Bristol Art Gallery possessing some of the finest, was buried here in September, 1845. I wish, by the way, that it were a more general practice of biographers to name the place of burial of their subjects.

Brunswick Chapel[9] is another of the Nonconformist places of worship which we owe to theological differences. It was opened in May 1835, having been built at a cost of £5,000 by seceders from the Congregational chapel in Castle Green. A red letter day in the annals of Brunswick Chapel is that on which the first marriage in a Nonconformist chapel in Bristol was solemnised within its walls. That was shortly after the passing of the Marriage Registration Act of 1837.

## PORTLAND SQUARE

Portland Square is one of the results of the speculative building mania which raged the city in the eighteenth century. A letter in Sarah Farley's Bristol Journal of May 1788 refers to plans for houses in this Square. Evidently the speculators shared the common fate, for in 1807 a London visitor described the "tottering ruins" of roofless houses in the Square. The Square was named in honour of the new High Steward of Bristol, the Duke of Portland, who, in 1787, soon after his appointment, visited the city to take up his freedom, and was received with much hospitality, the Mayor, Mr. George Daubeny, being voted £350 to cover the expenditure on a banquet and ball given on the occasion.

---

[8] The gravestone is illustrated in "TO-DAY" 4th Ed., plate 108; it was restored by the Bristol Archaeological Committee in 1963. The same group of history-conscious Bristolians erected the indicator to Latimer's grace, as seen in "FASHION", plate 101. A biography of John Latimer appears in "1950–1953", pp. 10, 11; the Latimer ceremony in the Cathedral is reported in "1950–1953", pp. 8, 9.
[9] This is now used as a warehouse. See the "1940's", plate 117.

In the centre of the circular enclosure the citizens erected an obelisk to mark the jubilee of George III., but it was evidently regarded as an inadequate expression of loyalty, and was quickly superseded by a statue of his majesty, the work of a local sculptor, which was described in the press as equal to that of Flaxman and Nollekens. The statue did not stand long, for after hearing one of "Orator" Hunt's fiery speeches delivered from one of the brass tables in front of the Exchange, a party of eight or ten men the next night (March 23 1813) went to Portland Square and smashed the effigy and it was never replaced. One of the men was sentenced to a year's imprisonment for his share in the outrage.

At No. 29, Portland Square, lived Dr. W. O. Porter, and there, in May 1850, died his sister, Jane Porter, author of "Thaddeus of Warsaw," "The Scottish Chiefs," and other novels which had great vogue in their day and are now forgotten. Sir Walter Scott was inspired to write the Waverley novels by reading "The Scottish Chiefs." Jane Porter was one of a brilliant family, and a tablet in Bristol Cathedral describes several of them.[10]

St. Paul's Church was opened in 1795,[11] and has long been the butt of architects, professional and amateur, for its "incongruous and anomalous composition." Originally Mr. James Allen, architect, was instructed, and produced a Greek design, which was accepted by the committee concerned, but, says Latimer, "in consequence of some occult manoeuvering, Mr. Allen was dismissed, and a plan of a so-called Gothic church, produced by Daniel Hague, an 'eminent mason,' was definitely approved. The secret of this intrigue has never been clearly explained," but at the time it was believed that the vicar of St. James's, the mother church, was the true author of the design with its "semi-Chinese tower." It proved a very costly church, and involved the newly formed parish in a 1s. 8d. rate for twenty years.

## BERKELEY SQUARE

Berkeley Square, of which I have written previously, belongs to the same period as Portland Square, and is perhaps the

---

(10) At No. 21 Portland Square, Edward William Godwin, famous architect and writer, entertained the young Ellen Terry. See the "1940's", plate 153.
(11) St. Paul's Church is illustrated in "TO-DAY", 4th Ed., plate 105.

eighteenth century Square which most completely retains its original character as a place of residence. True, there are a hotel, a club, and a school in the Square, but there are still left a fair number of private dwellings occupied by well-known citizens.[12] Two ex-Lord Mayors live there—Sir Frank Wills and Alderman Sir Ernest H. Cook. "The upper stories of the houses," says an old guide, "command a view of the great part of the city and adjacent country; and in a clear day Devonshire Place, near Holloway, Bath" may be seen. I wonder if that be true to-day.

## ST. JAMES'S SQUARE

To meet the demand of a growing population in the early years of the eighteenth century building began in the north and west beyond the line of the old city walls. St. James's Square was started about 1707 and completed within ten years. Good houses in the style of the period—Queen Anne's—were erected and well-to-do merchants and others took them as fast as they were ready for occupation. These houses remain to this day, though the Square has long ceased to be fashionable as a place of residence.[13] The Y.M.C.A. uses one or two of the houses, and some others are factories and offices. There is an entrance from Milk Street which is not generally known in the city at large.[14]

Tradition says that Mrs. Damaris Daniel lived in the Square, and there received as guests Defoe and Alexander Selkirk when the latter came to Bristol after his rescue by Captain Woodes Rogers from a lonely life on an otherwise uninhabited island, and so we got Defoe's immortal romance "Robinson Crusoe." The story was made one of the scenes of the Bristol Pageant,[15] and the performer who played the part of Selkirk was one of the most popular figures during the run of the Pageant, both in Bristol and in London, his picture appearing in many of the papers. No satisfactory evidence has yet been brought to light

---

(12) The houses in Berkeley Square are now mainly offices or devoted to University activities, even a commercial use. The number of private residences (including the Vicarage) has dropped to six, and several of these are flats. See "TO-DAY", 4th Ed., plates 82, 83.

(13) The last days of St. James's Square are illustrated in "1950–1953", plates 120, 150. Despite protests, the surviving houses disappeared in 1967 in favour of the widened Inner Circuit Road, and an immense office development.

(14) This, St. James's Square Avenue, is illustrated in "1953–1956", plate 51.

(15) Another reference to the 1924 happening.

that Defoe and Selkirk ever met at all in Bristol, but it is such a nice probable story that even Bath has claimed to have been the place of such meeting.

## KING SQUARE

King Square was laid out about the middle of the eighteenth century, and was first called "The New Square." It is stated that No. 18 was built by Mr. Ash, a rich merchant, at a cost of £3,000. The whole neighbourhood of the Square shows that at one time wealthy people must have resided there. St. Philip's Rectory is a house typical of the period in which the Square was built. Dighton Street, named after a once influential family, possesses one remarkably fine house which is now used as a convent.[16]

One of the houses in the Square now part of a boot and shoe factory[17] was bought by the Corporation for £1,070, and opened in March 1877 as a branch library for the residents of North Bristol. The premises continued to be so used until the more commodious building was opened in Cheltenham Road in 1901.[18] This library was to have cost £8,000; it actually cost £11,400, but the extensive use to which it is put fully justifies all the expense.

On the occasion of his last visit to Bristol in July and August 1790 John Wesley, then in his 87th year, preached in the afternoon near King Square, having preached in his chapel in the morning, but having no assistant there he records "so I was obliged to shorten the service within the compass of three hours." Charles Wesley, who resided in Charles Street, St. James's, from the date of his marriage, 1749, to 1771, frequently entertained his brother when he came to Bristol to preach. King Square was one of John Wesley's favourite pitches.

"My voice was weak when I preached at Prince's Street in the morning," says Wesley in his Journal under date Sunday, September 9th 1770. It was stronger at two in the afternoon, whilst I was preaching under the Sycamore tree in Kingswood; and strongest of all at five in the evening, when we assembled near King's Square, in Bristol." And again a month later he

---

(16) This has been converted into town flats.
(17) This is seen in "1914–1900", plate 78.
(18) The Cheltenham Road Library (later blitzed) is seen in "1914–1900", plate 149.

had been "weak and weary, hardly able to speak" in the morning. In the afternoon he was preaching at Kingswood to children and then adults, and "a little before five I began at the Square, and found no want of strength."

On another occasion about the same time: "In the afternoon I preached in St. James's Barton, to a huge multitude, and all were still as night."

Chapter 16

# ALONG THE BANKS OF THE FROME

**Plates 54, 55 and 56**

The River Frome, or Froom as it used almost invariably to be
spelt, rises in Gloucestershire at Doddington and Rangeworthy,
spots not far from Tetbury, and runs through Iron Acton,
Hambrook, and Frenchay to Stoke, where it picks up a stream
from the park and proceeds slowly through Stapleton and
Baptist Mills, along the Ropewalk, the Broad and Narrow Weir,
Merchant Street, Fairfax Street, under Union Street and the
sites of Messrs. J. S. Fry and Sons' factories,[1] the Central
Police Station, Rupert Street, and Colston Avenue, to join the
Avon in the Floating Harbour in a line with Prince's Street
Bridge.  A hundred years ago the river was considered to enter
the city as it passed under Wade Street (Traitor's) Bridge.

In the sixth edition of Joseph Mathews's Bristol Guide,
compiled just 100 years ago, it is stated that "over this little but
useful river there are thirteen bridges in the city and suburbs."
Their names are given, viz.: The Drawbridge, St. Giles's
(Stone), St. John's, Bridewell, Needless, Pithay, Union, Merchant, Philadelphia, Ellbridge Penn, and Traitor's—"all one-
arch bridges of stone."  The gradual covering over of sections
of the river since that guide was written has obliterated most of
these bridges.

In my notes on the Frome I start at the heart of the city and
go up-stream, calling attention to many of the streets and
buildings along the route, some of them of historic interest,

---

[1] **Frys moved to Keynsham in the mid-1930's.**

hardly any with architectural features calling for enthusiastic approval.

Writing about the river two years ago I described its condition in the "good old days" when there were no fads about sanitation. Then the banks of the Rivers Avon and Frome were even more filthy and stinking than the streets, and that was saying something. Frequently a street, or a portion of it, might be cleared of filth, but the river banks were left for the occasional disastrous storm to cleanse.

The Corporation sometimes became zealous and took action as, for instance, in 1700, when at a cost of £121 they obtained Parliamentary powers to fine glass-makers, copper-smelters, and other manufacturers for throwing refuse into the rivers which, the preamble of the Act stated, were being used to receive most of the ashes and filth of the city! One wonders how much fining was done, for there was evidently little or no improvement, and it must not be forgotten that for generations afterwards the Corporation allowed the city's sewage to go into the Harbour. Indeed, it goes into the Avon still.[2]

There was a great flood in the Frome in May 1720, Earl's Mead (a name which survives in Pennywell Road) being several feet under water. It rose to the height of the wall at the Ducking Stool, while Broadmead and Merchant Street were flooded for several hours. The Ducking Stool, originally designed for "short weight" tradesmen, became the acknowledged instrument for the punishment of scolds.

During the summer of 1731 the Council made new sluices "at St. James's Mills for the better venting of the water in great freshes" in the Frome, one of the earliest recorded civic flood prevention measures of any importance. The work was a costly one, the bill being £337 12s. 6d.

Both rivers greatly overflowed their banks on January 10th 1738, on account of persistent rains and an abnormal tide, and again just a year later. Each time much damage was done in the low-lying parts of the city, that of the first flood being estimated at £100,000. As, however, that figure appeared only in a London newspaper report, it may have been exaggerated. The second of these floods undermined two houses in The Shambles (Bridge Street), and they collapsed.

---

[2] Costly, post-war, schemes of sewage disposal are, at last, removing this health hazard from the Avon.

These floods must have been of constant occurrence through the centuries, growing worse as the Frome became more contracted through covering over for street making and other purposes. There was a disastrous flooding of the Broadmead area again on November 9th 1800.

Up to the year 1899 there were recurring floods from the Frome. Then an Act was obtained to make a relief culvert in addition to the works executed under an Act passed in 1887, and now after an expenditure of nearly £80,000 on works, and the establishment of vigilant supervision of the river, the city is quite free from this old trouble.

The biggest flood in recent years was that of March 8th and 9th 1889,[3] when there was nearly five feet of water in Broadmead, and boats were used to communicate with citizens imprisoned in their upper rooms. In all some 2,700 families suffered loss, and a Relief Fund of over £11,000 was raised.

On a good plan of the city of about a century ago it is easy to trace the course of the River Frome through the streets from Earl's Mead to the south end of Rupert Street, where it formed part of the Floating Harbour. Several bridges crossed the river between the two points, and one of them was the Drawbridge at St. Augustine's Parade.

The Frome Gate exists no longer. It stood at the Christmas Street end of a bridge crossing the river leading from St. John's Gate. As we have been reminded in the recent Pageant, the Frome Gate was an important strategic part of the city's defence. It was at this gate that Dorothy Hazard made such a plucky effort to resist the Royalist forces when they had broken through the rampart at the top of Park Street, as the spot is to-day. That was the principal way from the centre of the city to St. Augustine's and College Green. The Stone Bridge at the bottom of Small Street did not come into existence until 1755, and then it was built mainly for the convenience of the congregation at Lewin's Mead Chapel—who included many of the Corporation—a new bridge (St. John's) was erected two or three years later. The names St. John's Bridge and Stone Bridge[4] still survive, but nobody ever thinks of a bridge to-day

---

[3] A full report of this calamity appears in the "1880's", pp. 35, 36, and plates 5–12.

[4] This came to view temporarily in 1952 (see "1950–1953", plate 2), but its former appearance may be judged in the "1880's", plate 2.

when they cross those arches. Frome and St. Gyle's Gates were removed in or about 1774.

Needless Bridge, which connected Broadmead and Duck Lane,[5] was re-built on a larger scale about 1796, and a few years later Nelson Street was brought into existence out of what was previously called Halliers' Lane.

A new Wade Street Bridge was opened in 1798, the first one having been built early in the century. The street took its name from Nathaniel Wade, a late seventeenth century Town Clerk, and because of his association with the Monmouth Rebellion this bridge, originally erected to develop his property, was called Traitor's Bridge, and was so known for generations.

There were long stretches of the river open and malodorous. As Alderman Sheppard said at a recent meeting of the Town Council, if our forefathers had had the requisite vision the Frome flowing through the centre of the city might have been one of Bristol's amenities instead of becoming, as it did, a menace to health and an eyesore. It was practically an open sewer at the beginning of the nineteenth century, and long after.

In 1910 the Rev. Charles S. Taylor, F.S.A., vicar of Banwell, formerly vicar of St. Thomas's, Bristol, in a lecture to the Bristol members of the Bristol and Gloucestershire Archaeological Society, stated that the boundaries of the old parishes were determined by the Avon and Frome, and except for a short distance on the north-west side of the borough were probably laid down after the Frome had been diverted from part of its course. The boundaries were fixed so absolutely independently of the wall that it is reasonable, Mr. Taylor suggested, to assume that they were decided on before a wall was built.

From the Stone Bridge before 1247, when the Quay was made, the river when it reached the site of that Bridge flowed southward and eastward of St. Stephen Street and Baldwin Street to the Avon, south of St. Nicholas Church, turning the wheel of a mill called Baldwin's Cross Mill, near the foot of St. Nicholas' Steps.

It is difficult in these days to imagine a time when the members of the Corporation set aside a day for fishing in the river at Earl's Mead, and made such jollification, sport or no

---

<sup>(5)</sup> For Duck Lane now read the western end of Fairfax Street (opposite the Bridewell Police Station).

170

sport. The fish were perch and eels. Latimer notes that just on the eve of the first siege of Bristol during the Civil War, when blood was already being spilt, the Council spent rather more money than usual on duck hunting at Treen Mills (Bathurst Basin) and fishing in the Frome. This sport was revived in 1646, with all its old-time festivities, which of course consisted mainly of drinking and eating.

After a long interval, in September 1676 there was a modest revival of the Fishing Day. Fifteen shillings and sixpence is all that appears to have been spent, but there is a reason for doubting whether that sum covered the wine bill. In 1699 there was another revival, which cost £5 3s. 4d.

As late as 1850, following an epidemic of cholera, which carried off 444 victims, the Inspector of the Board of Health came to Bristol (at the request of the Council, be it said to their credit) and inquired into the city's sanitation. His report was a terrible exposure of inefficiency. The Frome he found to be a large sewer into which scores of small sewers emptied. And the evil was not confined to the lower parts of the city. "In a field in front of West Clifton Terrace," he said, "the sewage escapes over a very large space. Hampton Terrace suffers materially from an old ditch in which the sewage is collected. From thence it finds its way to the Froom." West Clifton Terrace is now represented by Alma Road, and the sewage was from houses in the Black Boy Hill and West Park areas.

A few years later three sections of the river were arched over, and thus new street surfaces were obtained. The first section was between St. John's Bridge and Stone Bridge, thus making some progress toward improving the approach from the centre of the city to St. James's Barton. The second section was between Union Street and Merchant Street, the result being the creation of Fairfax Street. The river had been passing under Union Street from the time that street was made in 1775. The third section was from St. John's Bridge to Bridewell Street, thus completing the thoroughfare which we call Rupert Street, though when Prince Rupert come to Bristol, in the days of the Frome Gate, the city was by no means unanimous in its welcome, but on the contrary, put up a stiff, if futile, opposition to his entry and did not mourn when he was ousted by the Roundhead forces. So as to make things right, the next street created by covering the river was named after Fairfax. In

1880 a further arching over beyond the Narrow Weir was regarded as sufficient for the time being. But four years earlier the Council had voted £10,500 to clear and improve the Frome between Wade Street Bridge and Ashley Bridge on account of the flood damage.

It was not until about 30 years ago that the Council felt able to arch over the section of the Frome between the Stone Bridge and the Drawbridge.[6] But after much debate, this greatest street improvement within living memory was effected. The dismal piece of water has given place to a pleasant little park, and the narrow movable bridge which had obstructed the traffic for nearly two centuries was superseded by a new wide fixed bridge. The last section of the river to be arched over is between the Ropewalk and Wade Street Bridge, which has lately been completed.[7]

Beyond that the river is still open, though passing through a thickly-populated area until Eastville Park is reached. Then and further up stream there are some exceedingly beautiful spots. One may hope that the Housing and Town Planning Committee will take care to preserve them.

We have begun well with Eastville Park, through which the river flows.[8] This land, 70 acres in extent, was purchased from the late Sir Grevile Smyth in 1888. The site and the laying out cost over £30,000. The river and the fine old trees are a great addition to the amenities of the district, which is becoming more and more populous. In 1905 an open-air swimming bath was added. Winter and summer alike this beautiful park is extremely popular.

But to retrace our steps. On the banks of the open river stood the Bridewell, at the corner of what is now Rupert Street and Bridewell Street, a site covered in recent years by the extension of Messrs. H. H. and S. Budgett's warehouse premises.[9] The site of the Central Police Station is over the river, and some years ago a mysterious voice was heard in the parade yard. The police looked up, but they were not wanted there. They searched the buildings without discovering the source of the

---

[6] This great work is illustrated in the "1890's", plates 23–32.

[7] In 1938 came a further covering over—from St. Augustine's Bridge to the present Neptune bridgehead, as seen in "1939–1914", plates 30–33.

[8] See "TO-DAY", 4th Ed., plate 121.

[9] Budgett's lost these in the blitz, and police offices have appeared on the site.

continued cries. Then somebody said, "It's beneath." There is, I believe, a manhole in or near the yard over the stream; the cover was lifted, and at no small risk to the rescuer a man was brought out of the river. How he had got there I forget, but he was probably engaged in some cleaning work and had been carried too far.

Fry's extensive factory site is underflowed by the Frome as it passes under Fairfax Street and Union Street at a depth which is not realised unless one looks down the flight of steps on either side of Union Street.[10]

Along Fairfax Street there are still some remains of the old retaining wall,[11] on which Narrow Wine Street properties rest. Turning a few yards out of the line of the river, we see the Merchant Tailors' almshouse erected in 1701 and recently vacated.[12]    The emblazoned coat-of-arms over the chief entrance has been removed, but the doorheads are there—not particularly good examples.

A little imagination and one can picture the scene when the home of the Dominicans was practically on the banks of the Frome and think of them as fishing in the Weir on Fridays—if the preaching friars did trouble about the larder.

When I referred recently to the Bakers' Hall[13] as one of the Friary remains, I should also have mentioned the Smiths' Hall. The Smiths' and Cutlers' Company acquired the hall in the reign of Queen Elizabeth on a fee farm rent of £3 3s.   An ordinance which was made in 1607 forbad a joiner or carpenter to contract to supply locks or other ironmongery. The penalty for doing this was 40s., and any citizen who sold or ground knives or tools was liable to a similar fine. It was this hall in which the Corporation attempted in 1610 to set up a new industry for Bristol, that of "Bayes and Sayes." They brought from Colchester a number of persons who were to be admitted freemen of the city without fee, and were to have the cost of the

---

[10] Now modern stores lining Fairfax Street stand on the River Frome.

[11] The demolition of the town wall is recorded in "1953–1956", plates 97, 100, 103, 179, 180.

[12] This became the Weights & Measures Office (see the "1940's", plate 109), and, since the war, a bank, its commendable restoration receiving a well-earned Civic Trust Award.  See "TO-DAY", 4th Ed., plate 107.

[13] This is further described in "HISTORY", Vol. I, page 81.

journey (£79) paid by the Chamberlain. That was ordered in
May, and in August six sums of £50 each were lent to the
craftsmen. The Weavers' Company much resented this competition with their trade, and made such a fuss that the Corporation told the bayes-makers that they must sell their
products elsewhere than in Bristol, and as a result the enterprise failed. In 1613 four of the men were forgiven half their
£50 loan because of their poverty, and it is doubtful whether
the other moiety was ever repaid.

As many as 23 trade companies or guilds existed in Bristol in
the year 1719, covering nearly every branch of handicraft. As
the city's population grew conditions proved too strong for these
companies. Their ordinances ceased to protect, and young
men would not pay the big admission fees for nothing. Some
of the companies were never incorporated. As a rule they were
poor and uninfluential compared with the London companies,
and so they gradually died for want of recruits. Their halls
were sold for other purposes. The Smiths' Hall was sold to the
Society of Friends in 1845. George Whitefield's congregation
had worshipped in the hall for some time up to November 25
1753, when he opened a new chapel for them called the Tabernacle.[14] "large," he said, "but not large enough" for the
numbers who wished to attend. In this building, still standing
in Penn Street, Rowland Hill preached (1771).

St. Matthias-on-the-Weir[15] is, strictly speaking, in Victoria
Road, which leads into the Ropewalk. It is a modern church
(opened in 1851) and the parish was formed out of the three
parishes of St. Peter, St. Philip and Jacob and St. Paul. When
the Corporation were approached for a site for the church
their surveyor valued it at £500, but being in a generous mood
they proposed to accept £150. Then the Lords of the Treasury
intervened on behalf of the ratepayers and the final price was
£300. The site turned out to be very marshy, and this fact
added considerably to the cost of the foundations.

That gaol-like pile of buildings the Weir Baths and Wash-
houses were opened by the Corporation in 1850. Churches
were springing up around, and no doubt the Town Councillors

---

[14] Alas, Whitefield's Tabernacle was demolished in 1958. See "1956–1959",
plates 54, 99–102.

[15] This church was demolished for the new road system north of the Old
Market Street underpass. It is illustrated in "1956–1959", plate 166.

remembered John Wesley's dictum "Cleanliness is indeed next to godliness"—his paraphrase, I believe, of a Baconian remark. This was the first institution of the kind provided by the Corporation, and it was thought that it would pay its way; but it did not. The recompense for the outlay of £7,000 and the cost of maintenance was and still is the increased health and happiness of the people who use the buildings.

The name Ropewalk survives and is likely to do so, though there is now no sign of rope-making in the neighbourhood. And there is now nothing about them to show why the Narrow Weir[16] and the Broad Weir are so named.

The recent covering over of the river from the Ropewalk to Wade Street Bridge (which has been superseded by an iron girder structure) has produced a long flat playground for the young people of the district who, however, still seem to prefer the older space in the Ropewalk. The covering has also converted the two streets which flanked each side of the Frome—Skinner Street and River Street—into one wide thoroughfare. The old names are retained, and a future generation may be a little puzzled to account for the two names, and especially for River Street, when, as will come to pass in time, the Wellington Road section of the water is covered over.[17]

In 1698 the Society of Friends opened a workhouse of their own to help weavers of their community who were suffering from a bad slump in the clothing trade. In this building aged and infirm poor were also lodged. It cost £1,300 to erect, and was later used as a school, the boys being taught to weave pantaloons. Manufacturing ceased, however, in 1721, and the place became simply a poor-house.

This building is now a mission hall, and is labelled "New Street Mission". New Street by the way, is become pretty old, but it has some substantial-looking houses in it, and one possesses a good doorhead.

At the bottom of Wade Street is a rather attractive looking municipal building—the Lodging House for Men. It is really a hostel for the poor, containing over 100 beds, and was

---

[16] Narrow Weir (which continued in a straight line from Broad Weir,—the river open, of course, once upon a time) is now merely a passage-way and disappears under a new 18 storey office tower and the eight-lane, foot-bridge-spanned, inner circuit road.

[17] There may well be a further covering over of the Frome to Ashley Road by M32 (the Parkway overpass), but not quite as Charles Wells envisaged!

opened early in the present century.  Here, again, the return is not entirely commercial.  The covering over of the river has increased the amenities of residence in this house.

St. Jude's, Poyntz Pool, is one of the churches of the district which were consecrated in the forties and fifties of last century— St. Jude's in 1849 and St. Simon's in 1847.  St. Jude's parish was formerly part of Trinity parish, St. Philip's.  Each building cost about £2,500.

At the junction of Lower Castle Street and Ellbroad Street[18] there was a ducking-stool for female scolds, on the north bank of the Frome, near the Weir, from ancient times until about 1784, though the last recorded use is in 1731.  The victims were set in the stool, swung over the water, and ducked three times by the beadles, who received a fee of 2s. for a first offence. If the same woman offended a second time the fee was only 1s. 6d., and in 1624 there is a record of two women being ducked, the beadles receiving but 8d.  At times the practice of ducking was suspended, not, I gather, because candidates grew fewer or magistrates more lenient, but rather because the stool got out of repair, for there are several references to the making of a new one.

Until a comparatively few years ago the Rising Sun[19], at the corner of Ellbroad Street had a picturesque exterior and ranked with the Lamb in West Street, the Stag and Hounds in Old Market Street, the Shakespeare in Temple Street, the Llandoger in King Street, and The Hatchet in Frogmore Street. The Rising Sun has been modernised, but I believe with consideration; the Lamb has been demolished.[20]  It was a good example of a seventeenth century inn with a quaint entrance enclosed by an interesting pair of gates.  Inside was a massive staircase, the newel dated 1651.  I am sorry to say that the best features, including a chimney-piece, were not saved for Bristol.

Redcross Street is stated to have taken its name from a red cross which formerly existed.  It is a faded street,[21] as indeed is much of the surrounding area.  We can see the remains of what were once houses of well-to-do citizens.  The Medical Mission,

---

(18) Now approximately the site of the traffic signals of Broad Weir/Penn Street/ Lower Castle Street.  See "1914–1900", plate 130; the "1880's", plate 99.

(19) This old inn is illustrated in "1914–1900", plate 127, and as modernised, in "1953–1956", plate 28.

(20) This is seen in the "1890's", plate 104.

(21) Redcross Street is now even more faded!

for example, founded in 1872, is in a good house which is well kept; in striking contrast to the house next door, in which Sir Thomas Lawrence was born.[22] That house is rather shabby, and might easily be passed without being observed, a workshop having been built out on the little front garden.

Sir Thomas Lawrence, who became President of the Royal Academy, was born at No. 6 in 1769. The house is marked by a tablet which has become rather shabby. His father some months later took the White Lion Inn,[23] and in 1773 became landlord of the Bear Hotel, Devizes. The old White Lion was demolished in 1865. Its site and that of the White Hart Hotel are now covered by the Grand Hotel, which was called the White Lion for some years after its erection. The elder Lawrence failed in 1780, and went to live in Bath, There the future P.R.A. showed extraordinary precocity as an artist, and while he was still no more than a child of ten or eleven years the fashionable visitors to Bath were crowding to his studio for their portraits. At eighteen years of age he removed to London, and in 1792 succeeded Sir Joshua Reynolds, deceased, as Portrait-Painter in Ordinary to the King. At once he became the rage, and nearly every family of note wanted to commission him. Yet though he had so much work he was always short of money. He was usually paid something in advance, if not all. George IV. once said he had paid him £24,000 without getting his pictures. "All the world is ready to employ him at £1,000 a picture, and yet he never has, I am told a farthing." There is in the Council House a portrait of the High Steward, the Duke of Portland, by Sir Thomas Lawrence, which was painted in 1790, long before his fees had risen to £1,000; portrait and frame cost only £149—picture 100 guineas, frame £44. The city also possesses the artist's autograph letter accepting the freedom.

There is mention in century-old guides of a Baptist Poor House in Redcross Street as well as one in Milk Street. The Redcross Street house was for four aged poor persons, who received 2s. 6d. per week. The management was in the hands of the local Baptist ministers or deacons.

The Royal Lancastrian School was originally the name of

---

the old "British" school in Redcross Street. Joseph Lancaster was a Quaker born in 1778, and the founder of a movement for the education of children of the artizan class. He started the school in London which became Borough Road Training College, where male teachers were trained for the schools he had in mind. The first Lancastrian school in Bristol was opened in a house in St. Nicholas Street in 1807, and it was one of the first half-dozen opened in England. Quakers were identified with the management of the school all through its career, the Redcross Street School being built and opened rather more than a century ago. It was closed in 1889, and the building sold, "free" education killing it, for when parents could send their children to school for nothing they did so in too great numbers to make it possible to continue a fee-paying school like this one. The last headmaster was Mr. John Henry Reed, who had been trained at Borough Road College. He started in July 1862, and was so young—twenty-two—that one of the Quaker Committee greeted him with, "Thou art but a boy". "I shall get over that, sir," responded Mr. Reed. "So thou wilt, and we'll help thee," rejoined the kindly old man. Mr. Reed passed away on the 10th instant[24] far advanced in his 85th year, active and full of boyish spirits to the end. For the last five and twenty years of his life he had been Private Secretary to successive Lord Mayors.

There are many men in leading positions to-day who received their schooling at Redcross Street, where there was an average attendance at one period of over 1,000 pupils. The school became famous in educational circles throughout the country. Dr. Macnamara is one of Mr. Reed's old pupils. At least one Lord Mayor of Bristol has come from Redcross Street, and many parsons, teachers, Government officials, engineers, and successful men of commerce can look back on happy days at the school. When the premises were sold in 1889 the money was invested and the income is devoted to scholarships for pupil teachers. A few weeks ago Mr. Sydney Reed read a paper to the newly formed Redcross Street Old Boys' Society, on the school of which his father was so long a master. I am indebted to that paper for these facts.

On the same side, and a little nearer to Ellbroad Street is the

---

[24] (10 July 1924): a reference to Mr. Reed appears in "1913–1921".

site of Redcross Street Baptist Burial Ground over the entrance to which is an inscription giving the name and dates 1679–1865, and an extract from the minute book of Broadmead Chapel stating that the Church agreed to pay half the purchase money with Brother Gifford's people at the Church now at Old King Street, to buy this garden in Redcross Lane to be used as a ground "where we might bury our dead without the ceremonies of the parish parsons in their yards." There they buried "the weak, but holy, lamb-like servant of God, Henry Hyman, pastor before Brother Gifford" say the "Broadmead Records." He was the first to be buried in this unconsecrated ground in April 1679. Gifford often resorted to disguise to avoid arrest for preaching in a conventicle, and for twenty-eight years endured hardships and pains of persecution. "The Apostle of the West" he was called, and many of the Baptist churches in the adjoining counties were founded by him. He figured as a rebel in the Monmouth Rebellion, and died in 1721. Bristol Baptist College received some of its bibliographical rarities from Andrew Gifford's grandson (1700–1784), the Rev. Dr. Andrew Gifford, of London, a Baptist minister, who was a great collector. Among his benefactions is the only perfect copy known of the first edition of Tyndale's Testament, octavo, 1525. A miniature of Oliver Cromwell was also bequeathed by Dr. Gifford to the College.

By order of the Home Secretary in January 1854, a number of parochial burial grounds were closed, and the following private cemeteries most of which were not far from the banks of the Frome: Francis's and Williams's, West Street (2); Thomas's, Clarence Place, Castle Street; Dolman's, Pennywell Street; Howlands, Newfoundland Street; Infirmary ground, Johnny Ball Lane. And only one more body was to be interred in the Quakers', Friars' and Workhouse grounds. In the three burial grounds in or off Redcross Street no new grave was to be made within five yards of adjoining houses. One of these grounds belonging to the Tabernacle, Penn Street, was scheduled by the Corporation in 1883 to be purchased for the purpose of allowing a new street from Redcross Street to the Weir. There was trouble because the Streets Improvement Committee declined to pay the cost of removing the bodies, and set on a gang of workmen about 4 o'clock one morning in the month of June to fence off the portion of the ground required for the

street, and to dig and cart away the mould.  In this process
bones of the departed were also carted away, and tombstones
were buried.  The result was an application for an injunction.
The Council apologised for the high-handed act of the committee, bought the whole of the ground for £300, paid £187 to
remove and re-inter the remains, paid the law costs, and later
laid out the part of the ground not wanted for the street as a
public garden.  It was opened in 1887, is nearly two acres in
extent, and is called St. Matthias Park—a most refreshing
resort in a rather dreary district, though to be fair, the lime
trees near, in the Ropewalk, are also pleasant to look upon.

Recent additions to the buildings in Redcross Street are the
school erected in 1900 by the Education Committee, now used
as an Invalid Children's School, and the Wesleyan Central
Mission Hall,[25] a handsome suite of buildings which have been
brought into service within the last few weeks.  This hall stands
next to the old British School.

Baptist Mills is a district popularly supposed to owe its name
to the fact that the early Bristol Baptists used to dip their con-
verts in the Frome here.  There does not seem to be much
doubt that "Baptist" is a corruption of "Bagpath", the name
of a Bristol family owning a mill at this place.  William
Wyrcestre in his fifteenth century Itinerary refers to a mill here as
Bagpath's, and the name had become "Baptist" on a Bristol
plan of 1609 nearly fifty years before there was any religious
community of that name in Bristol.  The first mention of
Bristol Baptists is in 1652.  They were an off-shoot from the
Nonconformists of whom Dorothy Hazard was a leader about
1640, and it is no doubt the fact that the early immersions
were in the Frome at some convenient point.

Another Baptist Mills fable is that the first brass ever made
in England was produced here.  The fact is that the Brass
Battery Works established by a company of Bristolians at
Baptist Mills in 1705 were but a local development of an industry which had been carried on in England for hundreds of
years before, and there is in the Record Office a reference to a
seizure of illegally-made brass in Bristol during 1638.  This
Baptist Mills works are now represented by those at Keynsham,
to which place the business was transferred early last century—

some time after 1814—the water power in the Avon being found more effective than that of the Frome.  At first the wire works only were at Keynsham.

The church of St. Werburgh's[26] stood between the Commercial Rooms and the top of Small Street until 1878, when it was removed to Baptist Mills.  In September 1879 the church was consecrated, being made as much like the old church as was practicable, with a number of memorial tablets preserved on the walls.  The fine tower dominates the valley in which it stands. St. Werburgh's is one of the few Bristol churches erected in the last 50 years which has its towers and bells complete.

---

[26] St. Werburgh's Church is seen in "1879–1874", plates 26, 30; and "TRADITION", plate 205.

# Charles Wells in 1895

On the great day of 14th October 1895, when electric trams were inaugurated, the second car carried local journalists and these familiar names of 80 years ago are mentioned: Charles Wells, Walter Hawkins, (Sir) Goodenough Taylor (died 1963).

As reported in "BRISTOL'S TRAMS" page 11

# Extract from the Journal of the Bristol Savages: "Grouse", No. 14, Christmas 1932

Brother Savage Charles Wells was a regular contributor to GROUSE, and several times he showed his appreciation of the manner in which his articles were illustrated by purchasing pictures at our Annual Exhibition, by artists who collaborated with him. Always a busy man, leisure suddenly came to him in a way we least desired, shortly after he was laid aside by illness from which he never recovered. He made a gallant fight, and the last time the writer saw him, a few weeks before his death, he talked hopefully of being regular in his attendance at the Red Lodge during the present season. Through his long association with the "Times and Mirror" he became one of the best known, as he was also one of the best loved, men in the city. His pen was ever at the service of any good cause, and where his personal aid was invoked it was given generously. The help he rendered the Savages was invaluable, particularly in the all-important matter of publicity and in the facilities he afforded our Hon. Secretary for the discharge of his duties.

H. E. Roslyn

# The Editor's Preface Writer

In 1974 Mr. Walter Hawkins retired after 54 years work on the newspapers of Bristol. He served for 14 years as Chairman of the "Evening Post", and a total of 42 years with that newspaper, which was founded as a result of the great "newspaper war". The arrival of the "Evening World" resulted in the closure of the "Times and Mirror", "Evening Times and Echo" and "Evening News".

His grandfather (Walter Hawkins), was an editor of the "Bristol Times and Mirror", and his father (Herbert Walter Hawkins) was the first managing director of the "Evening Post", when it was launched on 18th April 1932.

His son, Mr. Richard Hawkins, continues the family connection as a director of the "Evening Post".

# A Reader's Commendation

I would like to thank you for your whole enterprise: the books on Bristol, especially the period of my childhood and adolescence have given me enormous pleasure over the years: they are such a wonderful reminder of the scenes of which one was part. I think your enterprise was, and still is, unique, and has become part of a pictorial social history with significance extending far beyond the bounds of Bristol itself : I can compare it only with the illustrations in the Strand Magazine, but these are still *drawings* and not pictures of actual life in *photographs*.

D. W. Holloway, Cumbria

# Addenda

Page 151:    The old Library in King Street is now used for the Youth Employment Office, and Motor Taxation is done at Colston House, Colston Street.

Page 172:    The stretch of the River Frome from Wade Street Bridge to Eastville is to be beautified, following the Parkway road works.

# The Origins of the Reece Winstone Publishing Enterprise

In 1940-1941, the writer realised he had photographed many of the historic buildings being lost in the blitz, and began making lantern slides from the negatives. Other subjects showing scenes that had changed (trams, ferries, fashions, etc.) were added, and by 1947, the number was sufficient to make a lecture suitable for local camera clubs. Then, a kindly soul (the late Mr. J. C. R. Nutt-Hamblin) passed on some of his slides of Bristol, taken in 1897, showing horse-buses and trams, and these proved much more fascinating than anything the writer had photographed since 1924. This gift inspired the idea of collecting Victorian views of "Bristol As It Was", as far back in time as possible, even to the dawn of photography. An early decision was to limit the subjects to photographs only—no engravings, drawings, sketches or paintings.

Soon the number of historic subjects increased to several hundreds, and eventually required some twenty evenings to project the whole collection. These illustrated talks were now being given to gatherings outside photographic circles, such as church, social and old boys' societies, guilds and institutes. The request came: "Can you publish these historic photographs in a book"?

In his professional work, the writer had long provided photographs for other authors, so that he was in touch with all the national publishers. However, not one of those approached shared the confidence of the Bristolians attending the lectures, and after protracted negotiations, it became impracticable to proceed with the idea.

In 1956, the late Miss Marguerite Fedden introduced the writer to her printers, The Burleigh Press, and between us a way was found to success: *Reece Winstone became his own publisher.* This meant, of course, taking the responsibility of the cost of printing, storing the books, and selling them to the shops. Valuable moral support was given by the late Mr. Archie Powell, the doyen of Bristol Historians, who wrote the Preface for the first title, "Bristol As It Was 1939-1914". In 1957, 5,000 copies were printed, and it was hoped that these would go in five years. Judge the amazement at a complete

sell-out in five months!  Such is the enthusiasm of Bristol citizens for
their native city.  It was necessary to move quickly to a second title,
"1914-1900";  then a second edition of "1939-1914", and so the
series developed.  To my present printers (R. J. Acford Ltd., of
Chichester) I am indebted for the stiff cover style.  On the next pages
appear short descriptions of the twenty-one books;  they are the
proud product of a "one-man business", that is to say, with the help
of a patient wife, and a concientious part-time secretary.

Acknowledgment must be made to the owners of the original
photographs who kindly agreed to their reproduction;  the various
friends who have undertaken preface writing and proof reading;  and
the confidence shown by those subscribing to the books in advance
of publication.

Over one hundred booksellers in Bristol, and others in the area
bounded by London, Birmingham, Cardiff, and Plymouth, are supplied regularly;  the kind patronage of advertisers keeps the retail
price as low as possible;  and thousands of readers with addresses in
Bristol, and in each of the five continents, are circularised periodically
with news-letters. Sales of books now exceed 120,000 copies.  One
London reviewer has written enthusiastically:  "No printed record
of comparable value exists for any other English City".  So, Bristol
becomes unique in the world for having more than 3,500 photographs
published, covering 1840-1975, and the writer finds himself the largest
publisher ever of Books about Bristol.

Two unique historic photographs have come to light—they will
have to be mentioned in future National Histories of Photography—
the writer believes the view of the Cork Tavern, Broad Quay,
demolished in 1840, was by Fox Talbot's first process of "Photogenic
Drawing", pre-dating his improved Calotype of 1841;  and Hugh
Owen's photograph of moving people (1851-1853) is the earliest
instantaneous photograph, pre-dating anything ever shown in London
Exhibitions. These are reproduced in "Bristol's Earliest Photographs".

## "BRISTOL AS IT WAS 1939-1914" (4th Edition)

The illustrations portray the city as it was 25 to 50 years ago: trams, Greyhound buses, Blue taxis, discontinued ferries, "British-French" and "Bristol-Brighton" weeks, Clare Street and Castle Street cinemas, College Green, and the Centre before the changes, scenes of the first World War, and glimpses of that remote period before August 1914. The preface writer is Archie Powell, Doyen of Bristol Historians.

## "BRISTOL TO-DAY"

### (4th Edition)

With 200 up-to-date photographs 12,000 words of description, the Preface by John Betjeman, it is the first Bristol book to be illustrated by natural colour photographs. It has two indices, and a two-page street map; readers may enjoy the book at home, or use it in exploring with the annotated map. It is designed for the resident, for the visitor, and for the exile who has not seen post-war Bristol. This new Edition illustrates vast new building enterprises; the Severn Bridge; Bristol's Motorways; Cumberland Basin Bridges; the restoration of the Chapel of the Three Kings of Cologne; new University buildings, etc.

## "BRISTOL IN THE 1940's"

### (2nd Edition)

All the 175 photographs were taken by the author between the years 1940-49, and illustrate the war and reconstruction periods. Of unusual interest is the first publication of a German Air Force vertical photograph of Bristol taken on September 3, 1940, and three accounts of the blitz written at the time. Vincent Waite writes in the Preface: "This volume recalls the many memories of the part played by the ordinary citizens of Bristol during the cataclysm of the Second World War."

## "BRISTOL AS IT WAS 1914-1900" (3rd Edition)

The Centre without the Hippodrome or the Gas Company, Queen's Road without the University Tower, but with the Queen's Hotel. 1911 Coronation scenes; Royal visits of 1902, 1908 and 1912. Queen's Hall (one of the first cinemas) and the Coliseum Picture House. The tram with a trailer; and a snow plough tram. Horse transport: Hansom and Growler cabs; Bus; Ambulance; Milk Float; Tower Waggon for repairing tram wires. Blue taxis; single and double decker buses; AE 1; a fire engine; delivery vans; motor brakes or charabancs; motor tricycle post office van; and the Bristol invention of motor cycle and combination. Charles Thomas wrote the Preface.

## "BRISTOL IN THE 1890's"

### (3rd Edition)

Donald Hughes recalls the period in his Preface; these are some of the 186 illustrations: 1899 Queen Victoria's visit; 1897 Diamond Jubilee Celebrations; 1892 Covering in the River Froom to make Colston Avenue and St. Augustine's Bridge; 1893 Exhibition on future Colston Avenue; the first electric and last horse trams; the building of Cabot Tower; many quaint street fashions, notable architecture since demolished and the rural appearance of the suburbs.

## "BRISTOL IN THE 1880's"

Marguerite Fedden sets the scene in her Preface; The Drawbridge (now centre Gardens); open Dockside (now Colston Avenue); H.R.H. unveils Queen's Statue 1888; Calamitous floods 1889; Roundabouts on the site of Lewis's; sheep grazing in Queen Square; Steam Trams of 1880-1881; Horse Buses and Cabs; Penny Farthings and Boneshakers; Whale on Show 1885; Chess Club; W. G. Grace; Last Town Crier; building Southville; Castle remains and churches since demolished.

## "BRISTOL AS IT WAS
1879-1874" (2nd Edition)

Frederick C. Jones describes the period in his Preface. A map of the 1870's; Avonmouth's first Dock; First Horse Tram of 1875; Decorations for Prince of Wales visit in 1878; The last Drawbridge of 1868; St. Werburgh's in Corn Street; Dean Lane Colliery; Dr. Doudney's Soup Kitchen; Shipwrecks in the Gorge; Quaint horse-drawn vehicles, sailing ships, and broad gauge railways.

## "BRISTOL AS IT WAS
1874-1866" (2nd Edition)

Vivian Ogilvie introduces these 121 historic photographs; a contemporary account records the mayor's ascent of St. Mary Redcliffe's new spire. The Blackboy Inn, the Stone Bridge, a turnpike gate ticket, Brunel's railway station, Wm. Friese-Greene at school, the Cathedral minus the nave; tall ships, long beards and strange headgear give the flavour of an era before the first horse-tram; 16th c. houses on the site of today's supermarkets. An 1867 map and three indices are featured. Archie Powell's reminiscences go back as far as 1872.

## "BRISTOL AS IT WAS
1866-1860" (2nd Edition)

Lord Methuen honours the author with his Preface. Written reports on the building of Clifton Suspension Bridge have 16 illustrations; how local photographic societies started in 1866; Drawbridge (1827-1868) and its watchboxes; White Hart and White Lion in Broad Street (pre Grand Hotel); the house that fell down in High Street (1865); Steep Street; Mary Carpenter and ragged children; Ellen Terry; Deanery at right angles to Norman Arch; Cathedral with only one tower; Clifton Down Toll Gate, Hotwell House, Stoke Bishop Post Office in a cottage.

## "BRISTOL AS IT WAS
1950-1953" (2nd Edition)

The cover, in colour, shows the Coronation Crown on the Centre. John Totterdill, sets the scene in his Preface. Visit of Princess Elizabeth; the 1951 Festival of Britain and H.R.H.'s visit to the County Ground Exhibition; Coronation decorations in the suburbs; gaps in Park Street; alterations at the Centre; Wine Street before the car park; building the new Council House; Civic Cross and Queen Victoria exiled.

## "BRISTOL'S HISTORY"
Vol. 1 (2nd Edition)

In 1924, the late Charles Wells wrote articles for "The Bristol Times and Mirror" dealing with local history in a most entertaining manner. Mr. Wells hoped to publish this work in book-form, but he was unable to do so. It seems a worthwhile enterprise to carry this out, with footnotes to bring the 1924 story up to date adding illustrations of "The Bristol that Charles Wells knew".

So a new Reece Winstone book has come about:—size $8\frac{1}{2}'' \times 5\frac{1}{2}''$; stiff covers in colour; 96 pages of text (about 40,000 words); and 26 illustrations of "Bristol As It Was" in the 1920's and 1930's.

## "BRISTOL IN THE 1850's"

Sir John Summerson contributes an enthusiastic Preface on the value of these old photographs. The photographs include:—The bleak towers of the Suspension Bridge (called "Follies"); old-style shipping; turn-pikes; Bristol & Exeter Railway engine; an earlier Bedminster Bridge; ruins of Bath Bridge; churches in decay; the Great House (the site of the Colston Hall); Elizabethan and Jacobite houses in High Street; rural scenes in Redland and Clifton; the cottage in St. Anne's Wood; rare portraits of Brunel. Six maps of 1855 show courts and alleys since swept away.

## "BRISTOL AS IT WAS 1953-1956"

Michael Jenner writes the Preface. Over 200 photographs, all taken by the author, show:—

The first big stores in Horsefair, Broadmead and Fairfax Street; familiar landmarks now gone include the Shot Tower, Cotham Tower, the Chapels in Penn Street, and Old King Street; Ridley Almshouses; Gospel Temple; Arno's Castle Colonnade; High Cross; Campbell's steamers "Bristol Queen" and "Glen Usk"; Hotwells without flyovers; towers and spires without sky-scrapers; 12 College Street and 12 St. James's Barton; Chatterton's Statue; News Theatre; Bedminster Town Hall; Bedminster Hippodrome; Mary-le-Port Street; Castle Mill Street; Narrow Wine Street; Fry's Chimney; Whitchurch Airport; Bath and Bedminster Bridges in their single form; wide open spaces still in Park Street, Queens Road, Victoria Street, Baldwin Street; old houses awaiting demolition in Stoney Hill, Broadmead, Old King Street, Merchant Street, Middle Terrace; building Union Street Bridge; "Scissors" Crossing at the Centre; and the Centenary Celebrations of the Birth of Wm. Friese-Greene, Inventor of Cinematography.

## "BRISTOL TRADITION"

Sir Nikolaus Pevsner, renowned for his books on Architecture, honours the author by contributing the Preface. This collection shows the historic city AS IT IS, completing the trio of such books, and uniform with, "TO-DAY" and "FASHION". 220 photographs, taken by the author, illustrate the annual customs; treasures of art and archaeology; examples of historic architecture arranged in chronological order; unusual features of the churches; "Bristol Emigrated"; beautiful scenery within the city boundary; and written material of little-known facts and fancies. A QUIZ is incorporated.

## "BRISTOL'S EARLIEST PHOTOGRAPHS" (2nd Edition)

Sir Hugh Casson, writes the Preface for these historic photographs. Starting with 1854, the 87 illustrations transport the reader back to the dawn of photography, with a view of Broad Quay taken in (or before) 1840, by William Henry Fox Talbot of Lacock. A daguerrotype of Redcliff Hill showing the stocks in position, was dated to 1843 after research by the author.

A photograph of the Drawbridge taken in 1851-1853 must have been secured in a quarter of a second, to stop the movement of the vehicles. The Dutch House is reproduced again, this time the earliest photograph of 1847. The bridge-less Gorge, the 14 Stars Tavern, Steep Street, Mary-le-Port Street, the newly erected Cross on College Green, upsets on the broad-gauge railway, shipping disasters in the Avon, the gates of Tyndall's Park (now Queen's Avenue), the Corn Exchange on Narrow Quay (demolished 1849), and the S.S. "Great Britain" being fitted out in 1844.

Interesting written material includes lists of Victorian buildings dated and attributed to their architects; three maps of the 1840's, and a chronicle of events.

## "BRISTOL IN THE 1920's"

Kate Wharton writes the Preface to the 187 photographs. Royal visits are illustrated: The Prince of Wales in 1921 and 1928; King George V and Queen Mary in 1925; The Duke and Duchess of York (later King George VI and the present Queen Mother) in 1928; the General Strike; the Floods of 1927; the building of Portway; silent cinemas; the first workhouse in England (demolished 1925); the newspaper war; "Fatty" Wedlock; Fear's Corner; Ada Vachell's work; and the first aerial photographs of Bristol. A street map of 1925 covers two pages.

## "BRISTOL AS IT WAS 1956-1959"

Geoffrey Moorhouse of THE GUARDIAN writes the Preface to these 255 photographs. The cover in colour showing the Queen and the Duke of Edinburgh at St. Mary Redcliffe Church in 1956; the restoration of the High Cross in Berkeley Square; Kingsdown before the demolitions; Cathay and other streets in Redcliffe; Penn Street Tabernacle and Philadelphia Street demolished for the Broadmead Shopping Centre; changes in Marlborough Street; Cumberland Basin; St. Augustine's and St. John's (Bedminster) before demolition; Campbell's Steamers; trip along the Docks Railway Line; McAdam plaque; Dr. White's Almshouses; Long Row; Jacob's Wells buildings; Little Paradise; Mill Lane urinal; 21 cinemas about to end; the final phase of the birthplace of William Friese-Greene.

## "BRISTOL BLITZED"

A full record of those eventful days of November 1940 to April 1941, when Bristol was on fire. This collection of 207 photographs is made up of those taken for the Civil Defence, the Ministry of Information, and local newspapers; extra material by the author, plus a unique photograph of Avonmouth by the Luftwaffe in 1940. The Dutch House is seen after the onslaught but before the Sappers pulled it down, the Scholastic, St. Peter's Hospital, the Princes Theatre; practically all the bombed churches: the remains of shops in Park Street, Wine Street, Castle Street. The sad incident of 28 August 1942 in Broad Weir is vividly illustrated.

The Royal Commendation of H.R.H. Prince Edward, Duke of Windsor, Freeman of the County of the City of Bristol, praises the value of such historic photographs. Queen Mary and three of her sons are portrayed in Bristol.

## "MISS ANN GREEN OF CLIFTON"

A rare book about Bristol and Clifton, set in the 1820's and 1830's. Ann Green's grave may be found in Clifton Churchyard, but the story of her life is a *FICTION* written by Ethel Winifred Baker in 1936. Yet it is the more fascinating because the locale and events are *TRUE:* Ann's home in Clifton Court; the building of the new Clifton Parish Church in 1822; William West's camera obscura 1828; the gibbet at the top of Gallow's Acre Lane (Pembroke Road); the erection of the towers for Brunel's Bridge; Clifton racecourse at Sea Walls; Cote House demolished 1922 for St. Monica's Home); St James's Fair; the story reaching its climax in the 1831 riots. These events are illustrated in the 45 photographs and engravings; footnotes by the editor to the 216 pages of text explain the details for the present-day reader.

## "BRISTOL'S TRAMS"

Celebrates the Centenary of Bristol's Tram system: the first horse-drawn vehicles of 1875; the electric vehicles of 1895; and the abandonment years of 1938–1941, when a German bomb cut off the power. This collection of 266 photographs features work spanning the reigns of Victoria to George VI. The cover in full colour shows the livery of Bristol tram No. 190, photographed by the author in Old Market Street in 1938. Passengers and BTCC staff are frequently recognisable; the patented seat, which divided in half to give a dry part to sit on after rain, is seen amidst other curious details. Whilst every photograph shows a tram, or tram-lines, the interest to-day often lies in the background — the Drawbridge demolished 1892, St. Augustine's Bridge demolished 1938, Morley removed from Bristol Bridge 1921, etc.

---

## "BRISTOL FASHION" SOLD OUT

# "NO PRINTED RECORD OF COMPARABLE VALUE EXISTS FOR ANY OTHER ENGLISH CITY"

## CORRESPONDENCE

The author is always glad to receive comments on his books, or queries on local history, and undertakes to reply to all correspondence from his readers.

## THE ONLY . . .

The only Author in the World, publishing and distributing his own books, to achieve sales exceeding 120,000.

The only Town in the World to have its appearance over the past 135 years published in thousands of photographs.

## SOLD OUT COMPLETELY

"BRISTOL FASHION" is the first Reece Winstone title to disappear; three others are in short supply and are not now being delivered to the shops. Any reader desirous of completing his collection should order from the author immediately.

## CALENDARS

Three subjects are offered: a colour photograph on a gold-edged mount 10″ × 7¼″, with hanger, autographed by Reece Winstone.

(1)    Brunel's ship under Brunel's Bridge. (The cover of "Bristol Today", 4th Ed.)

(2)    The Royal Visit to St. Mary Redcliffe. (The cover of "Bristol As It Was 1956–1959")

(3)    A Bristol Tram. (The cover of "Bristol's Trams")

Each calendar costs 50p, post free, to any address in the world. Please state whether No. 1, No. 2 or No. 3 is required.

**Please use order form at the end of this book.**

# OVER 120,000 REECE WINSTONE BRISTOL BOOKS SOLD

## LIST OF SUBSCRIBERS

The following have generously subscribed in advance for copies of this book:—

Andersons Rubber Co., Ltd.
The Arcade Jewellers
Audio-Bristol Ltd.
Averys of Bristol Ltd.
Baileys Stores Ltd.
Bristol Blind Company
County Tyres Ltd.
Cumberland Welding Co. Ltd.
W. J. Farvis & Sons Ltd.

Hobbs Quarries Ltd.
House of Lewis Ltd.
The Society of Merchant Venturers
Stone & Co. Ltd.
The Unicorn Hotel
Uppington & Son Ltd.
Wilcot (Parent) Co. Ltd.
Wickham & Norris Ltd.

Yeoman, Serle & Co.

## COPIES

Copies of this book, or of individual photographs may be obtained from the author and Publisher.

The illustrations in this volume bring the total published in Reece Winstone books to 3,534. Have you them all?

## COPYRIGHT

Copies of the author's books are deposited at the Copyright Offices of the British Museum, and the Oxford, Cambridge, Edinburgh, Aberystwyth and Dublin Universities.

## S.S. "GREAT BRITAIN" BRISTOL COMMITTEE

As a member of this local committee, formed to ensure Brunel's ship stays in Bristol, the author circularised his 4,000 readers, appealing for their help. He is very pleased to report that the amount of funds sent to the Project Fund, at the time of going to press, exceeds £120.

## "CHANGES IN THE FACE OF BRISTOL"

These now occur so rapidly that the compiling of a written record of dates becomes essential. The author has produced News Sheets for the years 1961, 1962, 1963, 1964, 1965, 1966, 1967, 1968 1969, 1970, 1971, 1972, 1973 and 1974 designed to be inserted in his books for future reference. Each sheet is offered to any reader sending a 5p stamp.

**Please use order form at the end of this book.**

# "Publication in Book Form?" as Charles Wells mused on 21 July 1924

May I be permitted a personal explanation?

This is to be my last contribution in Bristol Street Lore, at any rate for the time being. Bristol streets are so full of interest that one is in less danger of exhausting the subject than of wearying the reader.

Fortunately, I have found many readers who have been kind enough to express their appreciation of these notes, and so have encouraged me to go on longer than I intended. A large proportion have been quite young readers, and that fact has been gratifying to me.

Will there be publication in book form?

I have been asked over and over again. I can only reply that I hope so. My hope is founded on the prospect—not too bright at the moment—of being able to find the time and energy to do the necessary revision. Years ago I used to think that as I grew older I should find less work to do. Now I can only suppose that I have not yet grown old enough to permit of the expected diminution. I shall have to join a modern Trade Union—one that insists on a six-hour day, and a five day week, for preference.

# Sir Neville Cardus
# "Full Score" (Cassell)

"The scene, the setting, immediate and adjacent, loom in memory. I am there again ... the flashbacks of time .... mysterious hallowed, cherishable."

THE GUARDIAN'S tribute to its great writer, Sir Neville Cardus: "He introduced people to sources of enjoyment they would not otherwise have known. He led his readers into unknown places and made them happy."

The Editor is sure readers will agree that the same remarks fit the writings of Charles Wells.